# Passing
# Seasons

By the same author:

A History of Long Sutton (South Lincolnshire). Produced privately, 1965 (with F W Robinson).
The Peddars Way. The Weathercock Press, 1978.
A Skylark Descending (novel). Robert Hale, 1978.
History of Long Sutton & District. Long Sutton Civic Trust, 1981 (with F W Robinson). Reprinted 1995.
Norfolk Origins 1: Hunters to First Farmers. Acorn Editions, 1981 (with Andrew Lawson).
Norfolk Origins 2: Roads & Tracks. Poppyland Publishing, 1983 (with Edwin Rose).
The Peddars Way and Norfolk Coast Path. Countryside Commission, 1986.
Norfolk Origins 3: Celtic Fire & Roman Rule. Poppyland Publishing, 1987 (with Tony Gregory).
Peddars Way and Norfolk Coast Path. Aurum Press, 1992. Reprinted 1996.
Norfolk Fragments. Elmstead Publications, 1994.
A Glimpse of Distant Hills (novel). Elmstead Publications, 1995.
Chasing the Shadows: Norfolk Mysteries Revisited. Elmstead Publications, 1996.

# Passing Seasons

-- -- -- -- -- -- -- -- --

## Bruce Robinson

Elmstead Publications
Wicklewood, Norfolk, NR18 9QL
Published 1997

Elmstead Publications, Elmstead, Milestone Lane, Wicklewood, Norfolk, NR18 9QL

First Published 1997

ISBN: 0 9523379 6 7

Text input and book design by the author using a DTP system with PageMaker 5.
Main text font: Palatino.

Printed by Geo. Reeve Ltd, Wymondham, Norfolk.

Front cover picture by Bruce Robinson. Drawing of Wilf Mannion, artist unknown.

# Foreword

SOCCER is now highly fashionable. "God help you if you can't discuss 4-3-4 and the floating winger at High Table," says the bitter don's wife in John Fowles' Daniel Martin. Famous clubs are floated - and sometimes founder - on the Stock Market, and high table at Carrow Road is set by Delia Smith, cookery grande dame and Norwich City director.

In the late '40s, when a youthful Bruce Robinson became entranced with the game, soccer was uniquely popular but not socially fashionable. 2-3-5 operated as unconciously as a Newtonian Law, as immutable as twenty shillings in the pound. The cuisine: a pie, a cup of warm Bovril, and titans with brilliantined heads and heavy boots, roared on by vast and good natured crowds. The game was followed from packed, Spartan embankments, and in the imagination via Press reports and the radio. Otherwise, information came in fragments subject, possibly like meat, to the prevailing rationing. Now - and one suspects, then - a distance lent enchantment. The transition within a generation from Carter's Park and the Happy Valley to rioting crowds is part of the story of this one man soccer journey.

If my own travels began rather later, the landscape is familiar and the conclusions similar. I first saw Norwich City as a small boy in the early 'fifties, captivated by the yellow and green and by Gavin, Kinsey, Hollis, Foulkes and Nethercott. Yet my first soccer heroes, when scarcely out of nappies, were Bob Hesford and Billy Price of Huddersfield Town, the club my father had followed from the Leeds Road terraces in the great 20s and 30s, and my brother from the bleaker 40s. As my soccer education developed, I learnt from Portman Road that referees were incorrigibly biased (though at nearby Layer Road I once saw the Colchester crowd give "Smiler" Dawes of Norwich a greater reception than they accorded the entry of their own, erratic team), and from an uncle, a long-time chairman of Bury Town, that it was not only feet that found their way into the boots of ECL "amateur" players. Bury, I need hardly say, were ever the victims.

This was a soccer world that Bruce knew. Yet fashioned though he was by the non-league heroics of the Tigers and the Tulips and the showmanship of Sam Bartram, the greater part of his period as the distinguished soccer correspondent of the Eastern Daily Press was to be spent on the featureless tableland of the Second Division. Across this plateau in the 1960s Norwich City wandered, seemingly lost between the horizon of fading legend and the distant skyline of ambition. City eventually reached Division One in his last season in the Carrow Road Press box, by which time one suspects that it was his view of the game's development as well as his own professional future that had undergone a re-appraisal.

Commenting on the affairs of the local soccer club is a foredoomed journalistic assignment, narrow, lonely, and ultimately unsatisfying. Excitement can exact a heavy price in routine and tedium. The correspondent discovers that he is the target of all and the friend of none. Alliances are formed and confidences won, but set against this is the endemic pettiness, the work of the watchful and grudging who think the proper location for the Press box is inside the club's pocket. It goes without saying, of course, that the reporter's judgement is wholly inferior to that of the most casual supporter. Next to the referee, a goalkeeper, and a failing manager, the lot of the local soccer writer is the loneliest in the game.

If this is the hour of the spin doctor, we can say that Bruce Robinson practised his craft with grace, integrity, and the manner of a good GP. Literate, reflective and phlegmatic, he was an analyst and essayist in a period when a more prosaic approach was still the convention. He recognised that the game, when played properly, is an art form and an important social phenomenon. He understood, too, the curious vulnerability and isolation of the professional footballer. His description of the battered and beaten City players after their return to a dressing room that resembled a field ambulance station, while outside Canary supporters were jeering their lack of "effort," should be read by every follower of the game. His account of his old hero Sam Bartram, lonely and unrecognised in the Carrow Road Press box, is a moving tale on the mortality of fame.

After sounding the whistle on his own soccer career, Bruce Robinson has won deserved acclaim as a writer of judgement and felicity on East Anglian history. In a sense this book is part of that history, and we are fortunate in our narrator.

Colin Chinery

# Introduction by Bruce Robinson

MEMORY plays tricks, and I dare say I have left out of this book many things I ought to have put in. But I have tried to touch the surface of what, for me, were the most important themes. And I have used lots of team details. At the end of most text sections you will find names which in a majority of cases relate to matches I attended. A word of caution, however. I have not given the individual match result, first, because I cannot always remember it, and second, because it is no longer relevant. In addition, some of the names may be wrong. They have been transcribed from cuttings, notes and programmes, and in most cases I cannot recall if injury or substitutions brought late changes. But no matter. They supply the flavour of the moment.

Special words of thanks to former EDP colleague Colin Chinery for his eloquent Foreword, to fellow Spalding journalist of the 1950s and long-term friend, Pip Spencer, for his assistance, and to Mick Smith of Spalding for the loan of photographs. I would also like to thank the journalists who helped and entertained me over the years, including former ECN Press Box companions David Dunn, Peter March, Dick Scales and Keith Skipper. And grateful thanks to the hundreds of players and managers (including Don Pickwick, Len Richley, George Swindin, Ron Ashman, Lol Morgan and Ron Saunders) and the innumerable club and match officials who provided so much excitement, anguish, and newspaper copy, and to the fans who coloured the backcloth to a great many dramas.

I would also like to mention the late CJ (Sid) Franks, former editor of the Lincolnshire Free Press and Spalding Guardian, who gave my interest in football a proper sense of direction; the late Frank Ward and the late Freddie Bolwell, who taught me about hot metal, type, layouts, flongs and newspapers; the late Ted Bell, former Sports Editor of the Eastern Daily Press and Eastern Evening News, Norwich, who let me loose on Norwich City and thus introduced me to higher echelons of the game; and Charlton Athletic and the late Sam Bartram, who started it all 50 years ago. I do not wish to contemplate what might have happened had Burnley won the FA Cup in 1947.

This is my fourth tilt at self-publication, and once again I would like to thank the staff of Geo. Reeve Ltd, Wymondham, for their help in providing a level playing pitch for my bumpy computer knowledge.

TO CYNTHIA
who endured the absences and
kept the home fires burning

# Contents

# 1 The Warm-Up
## 1947-1955

▬ ▬ ▬ ▬ ▬ ▬ ▬ ▬

During those depressingly grey, utilitarian years immediately following the Second World War, as politicians and power brokers bickered and shaped a brave new world hopefully free of conflict, ordinary families took lots of little decisions, just as far-reaching in their way. My family moved the wireless set from the living-room back into the front room. I say "back" because the wireless had been in the front room in the late 1930s but had been moved to the top of the bureau, near the dining table, to enable us to listen to the Six O'clock News on the BBC Home Service while having our evening meal. As in so many other homes, it had been a family ritual throughout the years of crisis. So the act of removing it once again to the front room - used only on Sundays, or when we had special visitors - was my parents' way of saying the crisis was effectively over.

The wireless was shaped like an upside down pear drop and made of dark, mahogany-coloured Bakerlite with a wavy line emblem (Philips, possibly) and restricted wavelengths which nevertheless proffered information and entertaining delights - Children's Hour, ITMA - from the Home Service and Light and Forces Programmes and such exotic sources as Hilversum. It also ran off mains electricity, thus eliminating a potential source of income gained from carrying accumulators back and forth to the garage, as many of my friends seemed to be paid to do.

Nevertheless I loved it, the short, silent interval of anticipation after switch-on as the valves warmed up, the crackle and static, solitary hours perched on the arm of a nearby armchair twiddling the knobs, engrossed, listening to foreign languages and unfamiliar music, trying to imagine the country of origin. It was my window on a world far away from marshland and the fields and the wind, away from the memories of a shockingly cold winter during which there were coal shortages and so much snow the roadside drifts were higher than the windows of the dark green Lincolnshire Road Car buses which struggled to take us to school at Spalding. And thus I have a very clear recollection, in the spring of 1947 at the age of 12, of being curled in an armchair in the front room listening to a football match commentary.

At this distance I can no longer recall what first sparked my interest. Perhaps there had been talk at school about the forthcoming FA Cup Final. Certainly there had been a lot in the News Chronicle about the impending, earth-shaking £12,000 transfer of Stanley Matthews from Stoke to Blackpool, and Liverpool's world record £15,000 bid for Morton's will-o'-the-wisp inside-left, Billy Steel. Or my interest might have crept in on a wave of patriotic pride after a Great Britain X1 (Swift; Hardwick, Hughes; Macaulay, Vernon, Burgess; Matthews, Mannion, Lawton, Steel, Liddell) trounced a Rest of Europe X1 (including Johnny Carey of Eire, Nordahl the Swede and Parola of Italy) 6-1 in front of 134,000 ecstatic fans at Hampden Park.

As for the Final, broadcast live from Wembley, subsequent reading suggested it was not a classic encounter. Indeed, some writers had the temerity to say it was a bore. But the details of the game, the noise of the crowd, the excitement, the commentary by Raymond Glendenning . . . something stirred my emotions.

It was extra time with the score at 0-0 and six minutes remaining. Then: "Hurst has the ball on the right-wing. He passes to Robinson. The centre-forward is going through. He's right down at the Burnley goal. He centres, a beauty, just over Don Welsh. Duffy is on it. He half-volleys into the net. It's a goal! Charlton have scored . . . "

Thus I became a Charlton supporter. Perhaps I was at a right age for heroes.

*Charlton Athletic - Bartram; Croker, Shreeve; Johnson, Phipps, Whittaker; Hurst, Dawson, Robinson, Welsh, Duffy.*

*Burnley - Strong; Woodruff, Mather; Attwell, Brown, Bray; Chew, Morris, Harrison, Potts, Kippax.*


If Austerity was the watchword then Rationing and Utility were its driving forces. Britain had emerged from the war in debt and clinging to the idea that it was still a world power. The reality was different. It was economically exhausted and losing its grip on its overseas' interests. As a consequence, clothes rationing did not end until 1949, a mere three months after conscription began again in the aftermath of the Berlin Airlift, though Stafford Cripps had introduced his scheme to establish the quality of basic necessities as early as 1941. The symbol CC41 - which was not replaced until 1952 by the British Standard kite mark - was a common sight on everything from furniture and electrical equipment to buses. It meant the items were guaranteed to last. But there were very few frills.

Life was a little like that for children, too. In Long Sutton, in South Lincolnshire, we had the wireless and a cinema, The Gem, which filled our Saturday morning matinee minds with images of Pathe and Gaumont News, Sabu and Tarzen, Gene Autry, Laurel and Hardy, Abbott and Costello and every conceivable cowboy known to Hollywood; there were concerts in the Church Hall and grass track motorcycle racing meetings at nearby Belle End, which drew enormous crowds; there were swings and climbing equipment in the Park; we flirted with cycle speedway but soon gave it up because of grazed knees and elbows, and damage to our precious machines; there were fairs in the spring and autumn and three or four circuses each summer in Cinder Ash; we tinkered with our bikes and cycled for miles, and explored the fields and connecting dikes for miles around; and we played cricket. But more than anything, and for hours at a time or until a parent called us in, we played football.

The regular pitch was on a field in Gedney Road now covered by a garage. Nearby, also endlessly explored, was an empty, dilapidated chapel and the old Army headquarters - or rather, a series of trenches and bunkers dug in the garden of the nearest house - dating from the early days of the war when troops were stationed there and armed sentries stood at the bottom of our garden scanning the Wash skies for enemy paratroopers. More often than not the field was cropped with broad beans, but for some reason the farmer always left a sizeable clear strip between the crop and the gateway. Perhaps he liked us, or more likely he needed room to manoeuvre his machinery. Anyway, there was always ample space. Jackets became goalposts, and as at least two of us owned footballs a kickabout at almost any time was possible.

No-one ever played as himself. We all took on the persona of someone else. Sometimes kick-abouts were delayed because of arguments over who was in which team and who was going to be whom. One would be desperate to be Raich Carter, another Tommy Lawton, Billy Steel or Wilf Mannion, while others argued over whose turn it was to be Stanley Matthews. Given time, it was invariably resolved. I was a goalkeeper, having grasped early on that 'keepers did less running about than outfield players. So I was invariably Sam Bartram. Sometimes I was Ted Ditchburn of Spurs, who I admired greatly because of his apparent ability - dramatically illustrated in newspaper photographs - to dive horizontally, which I used to practice. But Charlton had my heart, so mostly I was Sam. Being a goalkeeper also meant I could prevail upon mother to knit a thick, green polo-neck goalkeeper's jersey, which became the symbol of my chosen calling.

*Gedney Road gang - Chamberlain, Street, P Jackson, L Jackson, Walton, Robinson, Warner, and others.*

Long Sutton Town FC, like Derby County, Newcastle United, Tottenham Hotspur and indeed England, turned out in black and white and were known as the Magpies. They played at the London Road ground, sometimes in front of the wooden grandstand and sometimes on another pitch closer to the main road. They regularly drew crowds of several hundred spectators, and I can remember fans standing two or three deep on duckboards around the touchline.

There was great excitement when the Magpies fielded a "foreign" goalkeeper, either Dutch or German, whose name I can recall but no longer spell. And there was usually a communal sigh of relief when Jack Jenkinson was available to play, for he was a most accomplished inside-forward and, incidentally, a fine cricketer. But the Sutton player I really admired was Freddie Watkins. Flame-haired and fearless, Freddie was the epitome of courage and selfless hard work, equally at home in defence, midfield or at centre-forward. Never once did I see him give anything less than 100 per cent for the Magpies, or later, Holbeach United.

The local soccer pecking order placed the Magpies firmly in the lower regions, along with Sutton Bridge and Parson Drove. Holbeach United, the Tigers, and perhaps Bourne Town (the Wakes), represented the next recognised step up (there was a regular flow of players between the Magpies and the Tigers: ie, Megginson, Watkins, Cyril Wells; as indeed there was between the Tulips and the Tigers), with Spalding United, the Tulips, on a slightly higher plane still because they attracted larger gates and had mightier aspirations. As for King's Lynn and Wisbech, Boston United, Kettering, and later Corby Town (the Steelmen), they were too big to contemplate, really. We left them to pulsate somewhere in their own stratosphere.

In a sense we were already nominal Holbeach supporters. Every school day we travelled by bus the 13 miles from Long Sutton through Holbeach to Spalding where we attended Gleed Secondary Modern School. Spalding boys, of course, were ardent and vocal followers of the Tulips. They in turn assumed that each and every "bus boy" MUST be a Holbeach supporter, as Holbeach were the closest rivals. The rest, like Long Sutton, simply did not count and indeed never even entered the calculations.

Three of us once attempted defection. On the day of the Tigers' annual pre-season youth trial match we cycled the five miles to Holbeach, boots laced around necks, shinpads stuffed in pockets, and "signed in," hoping for a game. I registered as a goalkeeper - the fifth of five young hopefuls to do so, I discovered later - and we hung around Carter's Park nervously awaiting the call to join in a somewhat fragmented game which was nevertheless being watched by dozens of club supporters. Midway through the second half my call finally came and, after being told to pull a shirt over my goalkeeper's jersey I was given a 10-minute spell on the right-wing. Never having wanted to be Stanley Matthews, and never having seen Bartram play as a

T. LAWTON ENGLAND

winger, I really did not know what to do except pray for the call to come off. The call duly came. We had to cycle into a strong head wind to get home, too.

*Long Sutton Town - Watkins, Mitchell, Carnell, Megginson, Jenkinson, Osbourne, and others.*

Of course, there were also homely pursuits. I had a Subbuteo table soccer set (one cardboard team red and white, naturally, the other blue and white), and somewhere along the way acquired a set of cards featuring the players of the four Home Championship teams. They were not playing cards or cigarette cards - at least, they carried no brand name or advertising mark of any sort - and I am not certain how I came to own them. But they were a prized possession. The players are interesting. **Ireland** - Breen; Gorman, Feeney; Martin, Vernon, Carey; Cochrane, Stevenson, Walsh, Doherty, Lockhart. **Wales** - Sidlow; Sherwood, Hughes; Witcomb, T Jones, Burgess;

E Jones, Powell, Lowrie, B Jones, Edwards. **Scotland** - R Brown; Husband, Shaw; Waddell, Thornton, Smith; Young, H Brown, Woodburn, Kiernan, Hamilton. **England** - Swift; Scott, Hardwick; Wright, Franklin, Johnston; A N Other, Carter, Lawton, Mannion, Langton. The missing card must have been Matthews. As for what happened to it, I can only guess that this most valuable of items was swapped for something even more precious. A tube of Rolo, perhaps.

There was also the Gleed School at Spalding where I became an utterly undistinguished goalkeeper for Jonson House with a fatal weakness on crosses and a disinclination to come for through balls. Unremarkably, many goalkeepers were weak on crosses and through balls in those days; goalkeepers could be shoulder charged, and usually were. Sometimes ex-League players we had never heard of, but who carried an aura of greatness about with them, would visit the school for coaching sessions. In this way we were shown the proper way to kick or head the ball by players whose playing CVs usually included Queen's Park Rangers Reserves or Crystal Palace reserves. My main memory of the school house matches, however, is of heaviness. Heavy toe-capped boots, heavy mud, a heavy leather football, a wet, heavy woolly jersey, thick, heavy shinpads, muddy shorts and wet gloves, and wet protective elastic bandages on knees and elbows.

And there was always the matter of the rivalry between the Tulips and the Tigers, which came sharply into focus with a local derby in the offing. It will be difficult for today's youngsters to grasp how large and overriding a matter it was and how central football then was to communities long starved of colour and excitement. Local match attendances were huge by today's standards, 3000-plus at Spalding, 2000-plus at Holbeach. Suffice to say the Gleed was regularly swept by waves of local soccer fever. For the bus boys, most free periods and lunch breaks were taken up by talk of the previous week's match, the forthcoming fixture, or the merits of the Tiger's Shelton, Moore, Saw, Alexander, or the pride of Holbeach, centre-half P R Wright. Or the Tulips' Clapham and Towning, Lumby and Hayward. At home we had scarves and wooden rattles and dreams of glory. You were either Tiger or a Tulip. There was no in between.

My real footballing ambition, aside from seeing Holbeach beat Spalding 11-0, was two-fold. One was to attend a live Football League match. The other was to actually see Charlton at the Valley. This dream may also be a shade difficult to understand now, but we had only newspapers and magazines to pour over, the radio to listen to, and cinema news bulletins to watch. Sometimes they showed glimpses of Cup Finals or internationals, but the film would not reach The Gem until late the following week, and even then the items rarely lasted more than a minute or two. We also

*Spalding United, 1951/52. Back (left to right), A Waterworth, C Parrott, B Bryan, G Towning, T Eaglen, T Moore, J Stacey, L Watson; front, R Skidmore, F Bett, A Robinson, H Sharpe, J Nicholson.*

caught occasional glimpses of famous players in films like "The Arsenal Stadium Mystery," made in the 1930s. But in the main the stars were remote gods who were never seen - at least, not by us - but whose status and form we endlessly discussed week by week.

My first ambition was finally achieved at Filbert Street, Leicester, on Saturday, April 10, 1949. There is a minor mystery here because in addition to the Leicester v Fulham programme I also possess a Charlton v Derby County match programme dated November 22, 1947. In my own mind I am certain I did not see this game, and must have acquired the programme somehow; yet my inky handwriting records a team change, Duffy for Hobbis on Charlton's left-wing. Did I actually see Steel and Raich Carter, Musson and Leuty and Mozley tangling with Bartram and Shreeve, Fenton and Johnson, Hurst and Vaughan? Alas, I don't think so. In any event it is the Leicester game which has stuck indelibly in my mind.

Leicester City, the form team, were big news at the time and this was the interim between their having sensationally beaten Portsmouth 3-1 in an FA Cup semi-final and their much anticipated clash in the Final at Wembley against Wolves. Such was the level of regional football fever that a special excursion by steam train was arranged, picking up at Sutton Bridge, Long Sutton, Gedney, Fleet, Holbeach, Moulton, and all stations en route to Leicester, and somehow I persuaded my father, who had never been to a football match in his life, to take me.

The train was thronged with fans, we ate our sandwiches in a hubbub of tension, and it was all hugely exciting. I had never seen such crowds before. A mighty river of people poured through the unfamiliar streets towards Filbert Street, and once inside we could do little more than squeeze into the back of a dark and cavernous covered terrace to claim a somewhat restricted view of a portion of the far end goalmouth. I assume there were about 40,000 there, for we saw practically nothing of the game (Leicester were coasting, anyway, and Fulham won 3 -0). And although Don Revie's name is listed in my programme (which I later realised was a pirate publication, a fairly regular hazard in those days) I am fairly certain he did not play. Also saving himself for Wembley. Even so, peeking above the heads of the crowd, I can recall some of Mal Griffiths' thrusting runs down the right. We also saw quite a lot of City's goalkeeper Bradley, and Fulham's Flack. Leicester also lost in the Cup Final, incidentally. As for my father, I do not think he ever went to a football match again.

*Leicester City - Bradley; Jelly, J Harrison; W Harrison, McArthur, King; Griffiths, Revie, Lee, Paterson, Chisholm.*

*Fulham - Flack; Lewin, Bucuzzi; Quested, Taylor, Beasley; Stevens, Thomas, Rowley, Jezzard, McDonald.*


My ambition to visit the Valley was not fulfilled until March, 1951, which was also Festival of Britain year. Once mastered, the travelling from Lincolnshire was comparatively easy, and accompanied by another 15-year-old schoolmate - also in his last term at the Gleed - I caught the train at Long Sutton. Once achieved, the confidence it engendered enabled small groups of us to repeat it several times a year, or as many times as parents and pocket money permitted. I can still follow the journey in my mind's eye. From Long Sutton we chuffed to Spalding, and then to Peterborough and King's Cross. Underground to Charing Cross, then suburban train through Greenwich and Maze Hill to Charlton. Step out on to the platform thronged with red and white bedecked Athletic fans, shuffle with the stream up the steps to the road, turn right over the bridge and then left into Floyd Road, and saunter with the throng past Sam Bartram's shop to the ground, which was just around the corner. I always hoped we might see Sam behind the counter serving in the shop, but we never did. I think we were home again by half past nine or so in the evening.

*Evans and Bartram lead the players in at half time. Charlton versus Cardiff,*
*October, 1952.*

For star-struck lads from Lincolnshire the Valley, and London for that
matter, was a revelation. After an early start from Long Sutton we would
reach the Valley in late morning and start queuing immediately, eating
sandwiches while we waited. If it was a very important match we would
be in the queue by midday. And inside! A tiny, wooden grandstand with
curious wooden roof arches, dwarfed by the huge concrete bowl of the
terraces. And the crowds! Forty thousand, fifty thousand sometimes, and
never a sign of trouble. There was even time (though with what ease I
cannot recall) to make use of what seemed to be the club's only facility,
the longest and dankest open air gent's urinal I had ever seen in my life or
indeed have ever seen since.

The first Division One match I watched there was against Portsmouth, with Jimmy Dickinson and Scoular, while Athletic had the charismatic Hans Jeppson at centre-forward. In an early piece of enterprise manager Jimmy Seed had snapped up Jeppson, a Swedish international, while he was in London for three months on a business course. Additional restrictions on overseas players followed fairly shortly afterwards, but during his brief London sojourn Jeppson undoubtedly kept Charlton out of the relegation zone, sailed away with the crowd's cheers ringing in his ears, and went on to even greater things with Napoli and Torino. Talking of foreign players, this period was also the start of the club's - or rather, Jimmy Seed's - lengthy flirtation with the South African soccer world, a relationship which introduced many fine players to the English League over the years including inside-forward Sid O'Linn, the lanky and indispensible John Hewie, who could play in any defensive position, half-back Brian Tocknell, centre-forward Stuart Leary, the hugely talented Eddie Firmani, Norman Neilson, Dudley Forbes, Peter Hauser, Ken Chamberlain, Karel Blom and giant reserve goalkeeper Albert Uytenbogaardt. It would be nice to think Charlton might be able to open up a similar supply line again.

A month after the Portsmouth game we were back at the Valley again, this time to see Middlesbrough (Ugolino in goal, Lindy Delaphena on the right-wing). By now, football was my consuming interest, fuelled in part by Charlie Buchan's Football Monthly magazine and the sports pages of the News Chronicle. And from then until now the Charlton result has always taken precedence on Saturday afternoons.

*Charlton Athletic - Bartram; Campbell, Lock; Fenton, Phipps, Johnson; Hurst, Evans, Jeppson, Vaughan, Kiernan.*

*Portsmouth - Butler; Stephen, Ferrier; Scoular, Froggatt, Dickinson; Harris, Reid, Mundy, Phillips, Gaillard.*


Ironically it was cricket, not football, which led to my first job. For a couple of seasons I opened the batting for the Gleed School, and for a short time my partner was another Long Sutton lad who subsequently left to enter journalism with the Spalding Guardian, then the poor relation of the Free Press and surviving on a tiny circulation. Deciding later to follow another vocation, he told me of a vacancy for a junior district reporter to work the Holbeach, Sutton and Sutton Bridge area. Thus in the summer of 1951 I was taken on by the Spalding Guardian, then owned by Westminster Press and housed in small offices in Station Street. There was a shop and counter at the front, a small editorial room, an even smaller room at the rear for the editor, an old larder used as the block store where the paper's library of metal photographic plates and wooden mounts were kept, and a back alley in which we parked the office BSA motorcycle. As for the staff, they numbered five: Pat, who looked after the shop, took the small advertisments, sold the staff photographs and worked the telephones, Peter Tombleson the editor, Mick, the senior reporter, Derek Franklin the sports editor, and myself.

Life was chaotic but exciting. Getting to Spalding meant daily rides on grubby trains, chuffing through Fleet, Whaplode and Moulton. Once there, I collected mourners' names at funerals, typed out wedding reports, growled nervously through the countryside on the office motorbike visiting postmen and parsons, wrote a piece about an iron foundry in Winsover Road, started to contribute pieces to the Ayscoughfee Owl column, and later drove the van to Peterborough to take the flongs (page moulds) for printing. I also recall interviewing film star James Robertson Justice at the Bull Hotel, Long Sutton, and even managed a minor scoop about a private visit to Long Sutton by the Duke of Edinburgh, who was staying at Sandringham at the time. James and the Duke were wildfowling pals, apparently. And if I'd had a good week, with not too many clangers, Derek would let me cover some sport, including the Tour of Britain cycle race when it swept through the area for the first time in 1952.

During the football season he was primarily preoccupied with Spalding United, but fixture committees did not always manage to arrange for the Tulips and the Tigers to be at home on alternate Saturdays. And there were always midweek evening games. When there was a clash I tended to be sent to Carter's Park. As Press man I had a reserved seat near the front of the packed little grandstand. The telephone for sending copy and the result to Saturday sports, evening, and Sunday newspapers was kept in a wooden alcove next to the old ticket office near the front gate, an arrangement which caused major complications as going to the phone, and the time spent phoning, invariably meant missing a goal or two or lengthy slices of the action. Later, Georgie Hicks joined me as copy runner. Whether phoning details of Sharman's goal against Symingtons to the Sunday Dispatch or Tootill's injury against Lowestoft to the Norwich Pink Un, Georgie, who worked in the Holbeach office of the Ministry of Food in Church Street and was thus familiar with ill-completed forms, was an immaculate reader of my scrawl. He would wait for my hastily scribbled 60 or 120 words, or whatever, dash to the phone and then reappear before the next batch of copy was due.

But it was tough, sometimes. The Eastern Counties and United Counties League management committees also decreed there were to be games on

Christmas mornings and Boxing Day mornings, and indeed, most local derbies were played then. So there were missed meals and missed celebrations and hours spent trailing about on bike, bus and train.

In terms of public interest it was justified. The magic of local football was still very much alive. Crowds were large and vociferous, local pride was everything and the football, for the most part, was naive, free flowing and joyous. Football League clubs with sides in the local leagues, like Arsenal, Tottenham, Chelsea and West Ham, regularly strengthened their A-team line-ups with senior players recovering from injury or temporarily out of favour, and there was always great interest in the team sheets for forthcoming matches. Thus in the earliest of my Carter's Park match reports of which I still have a cutting, dated April 25, 1952, I was able to say that Notts County fielded four players with first team experience. County, incidentally, were occasional visitors to Carter's Park, and I can remember international Eric Houghton coming with them. There was also an emerging interest in soccer tactics, at a time when most sides were still playing the traditional 2-3-5 formation, enshrined in a comment that the Notts County attack - they were at Carter's Park in a Holbeach Invitation Cup match, incidentally - had a "curious inverted V-shape line-up." Whether this meant two withdrawn wingers or, Revie-like, with a withdrawn centre-forward, I cannot remember.

*Holbeach United - Anderson; Moore, Hargrave; Tootill, Wright, Fox; Nicholson, Price, Watkins, Megginson, Upson.*

*Notts County X1- R Smith; Groome, Crookshanks; Sewell, V Smith, Loxley; Mitchell, Brunt, Jackson, Broadbent, Brown.*

Today's youngsters who absorb most of their football from the tabloid Press or television playbacks, rather than by kicking a ball around for hours on end, can have little concept of the overwhelming sense of community the game engendered, particularly at its lower levels. There was a tight bond of allegiance to the local club, involving players and supporters, and hype was not only largely unknown it was, frankly, unnecessary. The fixture list and publication of the teams was enough to whet the appetite. Attendances spoke for themselves - 2000-plus at Holbeach and 3000-plus at Spalding. If the Tigers were playing the Tulips then the main A151 road between the two towns would be thronged with cars and buses decorated with scarves, flags and streamers and packed with singing fans waving rattles and bells and wearing rosettes and decorated hats.

*Hurst waits for Fenton's throw-in. But just look at the size of the terraces! Charlton versus Cardiff, October, 1952.*

The Tigers always took the field at Carter's Park with the booming strains of "Tiger Rag" echoing from the loudspeakers, and on one occasion, deciding the record was becoming worn and distorted after many years of use, a couple of us dipped into our pockets to buy the club a new recording. Holbeach fans, on seeing someone balloon the ball high over the touchline, also had curious a tradition of shouting "Billingborough!. . . " in unison and derision. Crowds elsewhere generally restricted themselves to, "Keep it on the island," but "Billingborough!. . . " reigned supreme at Carter's Park. I was never able to discover why, and older fans could not remember. It must have been an echo of some forgotten encounter when the ball spent more time out of touch than on the pitch.

Remember, this was the game's age of innocence, a time locked in memory, a pleasant pause before 1960s and 1970s hooligans turned Football League terraces into a shambles, before a few defeats released a flood tide of manager-bashing, and before parents screamed touchline abuse at match officials, and their own 11-year-old off-spring, who were merely wanting to enjoy themselves. And like innocence, of course, it was eventually lost.

Spalding in the early years of the 1950s had a shabby, almost unloved atmosphere. It looked and felt careworn. Most of the pubs were dull and generally unwelcoming, and there was even a tired proposal at one point to put a concrete lid on a stretch of the river Welland, also unloved and unkept, to provide the town with extra car parking places. The British Restaurant in the Sheep Market, which thankfully dispensed cheap lunches, was still open - as late as January, 1951, the general meat ration was cut to 8d a week, and food rationing as a whole did not end until 1954 - but there was little for youngsters to do other than go to the cinema (a choice of the Odeon, Savoy or the Regent), haunt the Fenland coffee bar opposite the Welland bridge, or "go to the football."

There was always work, of course. My job one day, using chalk and a piece of cardboard, was to maintain a display in the Guardian's shop window giving the latest score from the Test match as Freddie Trueman ripped into India's batting - he took nine wickets as India were bowled out for 58 and 82 - while the others listened to the commentary on a radio in the editorial room and shouted out the score. A year or two later the Spalding Guardian was taken over by EMAP. Our little office was closed and everyone moved across the Sheep Market to share accommodation with the Lincolnshire Free Press. At least there was the advantage of a small car park near the rear print works' entrance so we could play football with a tennis ball during tea breaks. Before that, however, London and the Valley continued to pull like a magnet, and there were long train rides at every opportunity and anxious hours in queues outside the ground.

*Charlton Athletic - Bartram; Hewie, Lock; Fenton, Ufton, Johnson; Hurst, Evans, Vaughan, Kiernan, Duffy.*

*Preston North End - Gooch; Cunningham, Scott; Docherty, Marston, Forbes; Finney, Horton, Wayman, Beattie, Morrison.*


The real attraction was an opportunity to see famous players I had otherwise only read about or glimpsed in cinema newsreels, and particularly, to be able to watch Sam Bartram. Sam towered over every match - he played in over 600 of them, or 800 if you count war-time appearances - was never out of a game, never had quiet periods. If he was not actually hurling himself at the ball in one direction or another he was standing on the penalty spot haranguing his team mates or urging them on. Off the field it seemed to me he was a quiet and gentle giant (see chapter 3), like three other famous goalkeepers I subsequently met, Sandy Kennon, Ken Nethercott and George Swindin. On the field, however, he was a showman, adventurous, courageous and colourful. It was not unknown for him to head the ball away. And I once saw him dribble the ball from his own goal line almost to the centre line, to the chagrin of his defence. Also, he dived at everything, perhaps on the basis that anything else was boring. Alas, he never made the England team, as we all thought he should, though I seem to recall someone saying he did appear twice for an England X1 during the war. More realistically, he had the bad luck to be playing when Frank Swift, Ted Ditchburn, Ted Burgin, Ted Sagar and Gil Merrick were still doing the business, but he was certainly one of the best uncapped English 'keepers around. More to be point he was a supreme entertainer and the crowds, myself included, poured in to watch him. Sitting in the wooden grandstand for the Division One game against Cardiff, and nursing the family's box camera, I tried to take some photographs of him and of the match. Half a dozen blurred images of distant players and packed, towering terraces survive.

Other important events were happening, too. Early in 1953 there occurred the devastating East Coast floods, then in June there was the Coronation, with all the implications that great occasion had for spreading the message of television. TV had been dabbling with sport for some time. The first trial piece of football coverage was Arsenal versus Arsenal Reserves at Highbury in September, 1937, and the first entire game shown live was the 1938 FA Cup Final between Preston North End and Huddersfield. Few saw it, of course, as few people had receivers at the time. What we did not realise in 1953 was that the Coronation had created an audience and a rapidly escalating appetite for sets.

Shortly after this I spent a week manning a Guardian photographic show caravan parked on the pavement in front of Holbeach church displaying pictures of the floods and the Coronation. And I was doing duty at Carter's Park on the very Saturday I was also instructed to trot back into the town at half time, to offices in West End, to register for National Service. I finally reported to RAF Cardington reception unit a month before Hungary (including Grosics, Bozsik, Budai, Kocsis, Czibor, and of course Hidekuti and Puskas) beat England (Merrick; Ramsay, Eckersley; Wright, Johnston, Dickinson; Matthews, Mortensen, Taylor, Sewell, Robb) 6-3 to awaken the country to the fact that we had slipped some way down the international pecking order. To be honest there had been earlier warnings - the success of Moscow Dynamo when they visited Chelsea, Cardiff City and Glasgow Rangers in 1945, and scored 15 goals in the process, and the USA's 1-0 defeat of England at Belo Horizonte, Brazil, in the 1950 World Cup. Perhaps we preferred not to notice. As it turned out, Puskas and his Hungarian maestros finally opened the eyes of a new generation of managers including the thoughtful Walter Winterbottom, and Malcolm Allison and the rest of the West Ham "academy."

Charlton Athletic - Bartram; Hewie, Lock; Fenton, Chamberlain, Hammond; Hurst, Evans, Vaughan, Duffy, Kiernan.

Cardiff City - Howells; Stitfall, Sherwood; Baker, Montgomery, G Williams; Tiddy, R Williams, Grant, Chisholm, Edwards.

In late 1953, in bitter cold weather and lashing rain, we were removed from Cardington to RAF Hednesford, in Staffordshire, for eight weeks' square-bashing. Even here, during the short weekends when there was time to get off camp but not to get home, football was attainable. Buses ran from the camp to Birmingham, which left Aston Villa and West Bromwich Albion within reach. I managed to watch Charlton at Villa Park, when Villa had Blanchflower in their side and Charlton lined up (at least, according to the programme) thus: Bartram; Hewie, Ellis; Fenton, Ufton, Hammond; Hurst, O'Linn, Leary, Firmani, Kiernan. But the big public attraction was WBA, who were top of the League, drawing huge crowds and playing like a dream.

The Albion forward-line of those days read: Griffin, Ryan, Allen, Nicholls and Lee. Left-winger George Lee later joined Norwich City as trainer, and we became acquaintances killing time together while travelling to or from away matches. But it is the regular litany of the five names I remember above all. It is ingrained, and unconsciously I still do it even when scanning a team sheet today. Griffin, Ryan, Allen, Nicholls and Lee. Hurst, O'Linn, Vaughan, Kiernan and Duffy. Delaney, Morris, Rowley, Pearson and Mitten. Canario, Del Sol, Di Stefano, Puskas and Gento. Hancocks, Broadbent, Swinbourne, Wilshaw, Mullen. Nicholson, Megginson, Sharman, Fox and Dwane. Matthews, Carter, Lawton, Mannion and Langton. Adams, Crook, Ottosson, Johnson and Milligan. They have a resonance all of their own.

West Brom were playing some sweet football at the time, as sides do when everything is going right and confidence is high, and went on to win the FA Cup in the 1953/54 season, beating Preston 3-2 at Wembley in the Final. So George Lee, a quick, orthodox winger who could have shown some of today's players a thing or two about crossing from the touchline, ultimately got his Cup winners' gong.

During that little portion of the season I also watched WBA against Sunderland (with Daniel, Ford and Bingham, and I think Len Shackleton;

*Charlton Athletic - Back (left to right), Jimmy Trotter, Fenton, Shreeve, Bartram, Phipps, Lock, Forbes; front, Hurst, O'Linn, Vaughan, Cullam, Kiernan.*

though if not, I certainly saw him later) and in particular, their 5-2 drubbing of Chelsea. Charlton, in third place in Division One and chasing the leaders hard, had been the only side to win at the Hawthorns that season. WBA's five goals against Chelsea made up for the fact that RAF duties did not allow me to see the Addicks.

*West Bromwich Albion - Heath; Rickaby, Millard; Dudley, Dugdale, Barlow; Griffin, Ryan, Allen, Nicholls, Lee.*

*Chelsea - Robertson; Harris, Willemse; Armstrong, J Saunders, D Saunders; Parsons, McNichol, Bentley, Stubbs, Blunstone.*


On New Year's Day, 1954, the RAF moved me on again, this time as a junior Aircraftsman (signals) to the Flying Training Command base at Worksop, in Nottinghamshire. We actually played football there, too. Two weeks' after arriving I played in goal for Signals Flight against Technical Wing. We lost 7-2, but somehow this was interpreted as an improvement for they had lost the previous match 9-0. There were several games after that, equally desultory and disastrous. One weekend a colleague from Liverpool returned to camp after a weekend pass crowing that he had seen Liverpool take on Charlton at Anfield. He gave me the match programme. Sam, nearing 40 at that point, was still there, along with Fenton, Hammond, Hurst and O'Linn. But Campbell, Ayre, Leary and Firmani had come into the side, replacing some well-known names.

We watched Doris Day films at every opportunity, of course, but our sporting focus was firmly on Sheffield, again because it was easy to get to by coach from Ranby or train from Retford. Once, when Sheffield United met Spurs, I went to the match in pouring rain, got lost on the way to the ground, later dried off in a cinema and missed the last bus, caught a late train to Worksop and walked the five miles or so back to the camp, finally sneaking past the guardroom at about 1.30pm. And in March, 1955, a party of off-duty National Servicemen travelled to Hillsborough to see England B v Germany B in a midweek floodlit match, only the second floodlit match ever held at Hillsborough and the first time I had ever seen it.

Football lighting was apparently first tried as long ago as 1878, but the first game in modern times to be properly lit was a friendly, Arsenal versus Hapoel Tel Aviv, at Highbury in September, 1951. It took the stuffy Football League committee another five years before they allowed League games to follow suit; but I thought it added a marvellous feeling of theatre to the game. There was also something dramatic and deliciously decadent about turning out to watch a match in the blackness of a winter's evening. England B, incidentally, included Reg Matthews in goal, Jeff Hall at right-back, the indomitable Duncan Edwards at left-half, and John Atyeo, Roy Swinbourne, the imperious Johnny Haynes, and Billy Kiernan in attack. Kiernan was probably the reason why I went.

We also managed to get to Bramall Lane on a number of occasions, watching Burnley (with McIlroy, Cheesebrough and Shannon) and Newcastle United (with Stokoe, later a Charlton manager, Milburn, Mitchell, Keeble and Curry). Sheffield had major problems with polluted air in those days, and it also had Sheffield Wednesday. But United had Jimmy Hagan, which helped make up for grime spots on hands, shirts and faces, and the peculiarities of a ground which, because it was also used by Yorkshire Cricket Club, had one yawningly empty and largely unoccupied touchline.

*Sheffield United - Burgin; Furniss, G Shaw; Hoyland, J Shaw, Fountain; Ringstead, Hagan, Cross, Waldock, Grainger.*

*Tottenham Hotspur - Ditchburn; Ramsay, Hopkins; Nicholson, Clarke, Marchi; McClellan, Baily, Dunmore, Brooks, Gavin.*

The RAF, at least at Worksop, had some reasonably benevolent leave arrangements, and with a one-week pass in my pocket I headed for a memorable few days in London, watching Arsenal play Blackpool at Highbury on the Saturday and Charlton against Portsmouth at the Valley on the Monday. All four teams are worth reprinting from the programmes: **Arsenal** - Kelsey; Wills, Evans; Goring, Fotheringham, Oakes; Clapton, Tapscott, Roper, Lishman, Bloomfield. **Blackpool** - Farm; Gratrix, Garrett; Fenton, Johnston, Kelly; Matthews, Taylor, Mortensen, Mudie, McKenna. **Charlton Athletic** - Bartram; Campbell, Townsend; Hewie, Ufton, Hammond; Ryan, O'Linn, Leary, Kiernan, Pembery. **Portsmouth** - Uprichard; McGhee, Mansell; Pickett, Reid, Dickinson; Harris, Gordon, Henderson, Rees, Raffety.

Memories of these games are shadowy, but I do recall the immense crowds and the thrill of being among them. Looking at the teams now they seem to represent sides in transition. Blackpool were finding the going very hard - for one thing, they were not getting any younger; Arsenal lacked the class and resonance of old; and Charlton, shorn of Lock and Fenton, Hurst, Duffy and the marvellous Charlie Vaughan, were starting to lose their way.

Another reason to rejoice being close to Sheffield was Hillsborough which, with its vast covered terraces and electronic scoreboard, was one of the most modern club grounds in the country at that time. In December, 1954, Wolves, League champions and League leaders, were the visitors. Having beaten Spartak, the Russian club, and Honved, the famous Hungarian side, Wolves' long ball game was justifiably famous. Major Buckley at Wolves and Herbert Chapman at Arsenal had attempted to modernise a reluctant game between the wars, and Bill Nicholson and Stan Cullis tried to do so again in the early 1950s. Nicholson, at Tottenham, opted for short, accurate passing and running off the ball; Cullis introduced a no-nonsense long ball game aped by Watford and Wimbledon in the 1980s. At this distance the Cullis format seems to have smacked more of a brilliant use of available resources rather than an end in itself, though Wimbledon fans, particularly, might disagree. Yet the Continentals, and indeed other Division One clubs, at first taken aback by the speed and breadth of Wolves' attacking, slowly came to terms with it, though this must not be allowed to detract from their achievements. For a time Wolves were the talk and the pride of the country.

According to my programme the Wolves' side at Hillsborough read: Williams; Stuart, Shorthouse; Slater, Wright, Flowers; Hancocks, Broadbent,

Swinbourne, Wilshaw, Smith. Wednesday seem to have fielded Albert Quixall and Jackie Sewell, two fine touch players, which must have provided an extraordinary contrast.

Another reason for our interest in Wednesday and in Hillsborough was the fact that one of the club's players, Jimmy McAnearney, was doing his National Service at Worksop. His brother, Tom, was a regular in the Wednesday side and we waited, hoping, for Jimmy to get his chance. One occasion when he did was in September, 1955, when Quixall was injured and both brothers were named for the Division One clash against Leicester City. Naturally, we were there.

*Sheffield Wednesday - McIntosh; Martin, Bingley; Gibson, O'Donnell, T McAnearney; R Froggatt, Sewell, Shiner, J McAnearney, Broadbent.*

*Leicester City - Anderson; Cunningham, Webb; J Froggatt, Fincham, Russell; Wright, Morris, Hines, Rowley, Hogg.*

# 2 First Half 1956-1959

■ ■ ■ ■ ■ ■ ■

Life in Spalding after life in the RAF seemed as glutinous as it had been before, if not more so once the novelty of Civvy Street had worn off. There was also the complication of having to move into digs - my first being a room above the bar at the Hole in the Wall pub - at the insistence of the then editor of the Free Press and Guardian, Sid Franks, who, despite the decision, really was the soul of consideration and a warm, responsible newspaperman of the old school. There was a sinking feeling of increasing isolation, too, for many of my friends of two years' earlier were either away serving in the Forces or awaiting the call to arms. The ludicrous Suez War, a bitterly divided and dangerously troublesome Cyprus, and the heart-wrenching hopelessness of the Hungarian Revolution were all in the pipeline; several lads I knew were involved in the first two while I, demobbed too early to be involved in any of them, discovered a tenuous link with the third. Four years after discharge I returned to Nottinghamshire to re-visit RAF Worksop only to find it deserted and in ruins. The Meteors had moved out shortly after I left, apparently, and Hungarian refugees had moved in until they could be found other accommodation. They had stayed only a few months.

There were compensations, it must be said. The journalistic work was busy and varied and for a time football took a back seat. I toured the villages to collate and write news paragraphs, wrote a feature about the Greenwich Meridian passing through Wignall's Gate, Holbeach - a spot later marked with a special stone - and was in the dusty clock room at the top of the old Corn Exchange when the ancient 23-bell carillon was brought back into life for the first time in years by an expert from Bristol. And of course, there were the Tulip Tours to be covered. These were forerunners of the now well established Tulip Parades, and involved the Tulip Queen and her attendants travelling a designated circuit around the flower fields followed by hordes of visitors and long lines of cars.

Earlier in the year there was also an appallingly bad winter to survive. Electricity and water supplies failed, villages were cut off and vehicles and buses, some of them loaded with schoolchildren, were trapped by drifts and blizzards in Whaplode before being rescued by villagers and farmers with tractors. Nevertheless, life went on. One week before helping to write news reports of the blizzard, I was at White Hart Lane.

Tottenham had been drawn at home in the third round of the FA Cup, but the big surprise was their opponents, Boston United of the Midland League, who had performed the extraordinary second round feat of defeating Derby County 6-1. Tottenham, hitherto displaying patchy form in the League, had nevertheless played and won 2-1 at the Valley the previous week, Charlton then standing fourth in the Division One table. So they were in confident mood. They also had theoretical strength in depth. I note from the Boston match programme that the Spurs' Reserve team attack against QPR Reserves a few days' earlier had comprised: Walters, Stokes, Dunmore, Baily and Dyson. Each one of them might have found a home at any other Division One club. And yet, unless memory fails me, not one of the five made the line-up against United. In any event Spurs won 4-0 and Boston returned home with their bank balance improved and their pride more or less intact.

*Tottenham Hotspur - Reynolds; Norman, Hopkins; Blanchflower, Clarke, Marchi; Dulin, Brooks, Duquemin, Smith, Robb.*

*Boston United - Middleton; Robinson, Snade; D Hazledine, Miller, Lowder; Harrison, G Hazledine, Wilkins, Birbeck, Howlett.*


Long Sutton were on the periphery of the local football scene, at least as far as Holbeach, Spalding, Boston and Wisbech were concerned. But they were ambitious and they did make at least one attempt to steal a march over their rivals. One autumn the club resolved to erect floodlights, initially to enable them to train during the dark evenings but with a longer term aim of actually playing a night match. This was new territory, but it was a prospect that thrilled player-manager Cyril Wells, who ran three teams for Long Sutton and who told me that two of his young Magpies had been invited for trials with Derby County and Wolves.

There were a number of problems related to the scheme - money and know-how among them. For example, no-one in the area had ever tried to light an area as big as a football field for up to two hours, and consequently no-one was certain how much it would cost or how it could be done. Discussions about portable generators and cable sizes dominated gossip. Then assistance came from an unexpected source.

Funfairs were a familiar sight and sound in the 1950s - Fendick and Gray being the most popular and regular in the town - and it happened that Herbert Gray's fair was on the London Road ground at the time. The fair folk heard all the talk of floodlights and the problems being encountered, and went to the club with an offer to lend a hand in an experiment, making use of the funfair equipment. The Magpies accepted, and on the appointed afternoon a band of volunteers turned up to do the work.

We toiled in pouring rain to drag heavy cables and 18ft poles around the touchlines, dig holes, and drag the poles upright. By the time the job was finished it was pitch dark, torch batteries were running out, and a group of bemused, wet and impatient club footballers were having to train in front of the grandstand by the light of a hurricane lamp. Finally all 16 poles were erected, six down each touchline and two behind each goal, topped by 300 watt lamps surrounded by makeshift reflectors, and the cables were wired in.

No-one quite knew what to expect. But when the fairground generator was switched on first the nearby roundabouts and swings glowed colourfully and moved noisily into life, then a gentle glimmer hesitantly penetrated the gloom around the football pitch. Some of the lamps shone at full power, some shimmered diffidently, while others were as dead as doornails. Cyril was delighted, for the initial feeling was that with different cable and one or two technical bugs ironed out night matches might indeed be played. They started on the work immediately, but this time I didn't wait, preferring to go home to dry out.

All this was a long way from Floyd Road and the Valley, but trips were squeezed into free weekends. By now Sam Bartram was coming to the end of his playing career - he would do so at the end of the 1955/56 season - and new names were beginning to show up on the team sheet. Though it was difficult to detect at the time, storm clouds were beginning to gather over the head of secretary/manager Jimmy Seed.

*Charlton Athletic - Bartram; Campbell, Ellis; O'Linn, Hewie, Hammond; Hurst, Ayre, Leary, Ryan, Kiernan.*

*Arsenal - Kelsey; Charlton, Evans; Goring, Dodgin, Bowen; Clapton, Herd, Groves, Bloomfield, Tiddy.*


In 1956 the Eastern Counties League, in addition to Spalding and Holbeach, also boasted Colchester United Reserves, Tottenham A, West Ham A and Norwich City A, along with old favourites and traditional adversaries March, Peterborough Reserves, Clacton, Cambridge United,

Stowmarket, Yarmouth, Gorleston, Lowestoft, Sudbury, Harwich and Parkeston, Bury Town, Biggleswade, Eynesbury and Chelmsford City. These were the balmy, best days of the old ECL, and for its resolute champion, secretary Arthur Rudd.

But changes were afoot, and not only in soccer circles where Don Revie's deep-lying centre-forward ploy was gaining favour among tacticians, thus beginning a trend which ended with shirt numbers becoming totally meaningless as far as a player's on-field position was concerned. Bill Haley's "Rock Around the Clock" boomed incessantly from radios and loudspeakers, signalling a gigantic shift in popular music tastes; Grace Kelly and Brigitte Bardot smiled and pouted from cinema screens and the pages of newspapers, and broke hearts in the process; there were plenty of jobs available, increasing numbers of cars on the roads, despite petrol rationing, and more fridges, electric toasters, and of course, TVs. And there was a new bounce in peoples' footsteps and an increasing awareness that, despite the Cold War and the ever present threat of atomic oblivion, things were actually getting better. We haunted Spalding's trendy meeting place - the Fenland milk bar - where we drank coffee in clear plastic cups, travelled further afield for an evening out - as far as Peterborough or Boston - and even contemplated a holiday abroad. My first ever foreign foray, to Switzerland, cost me £37 for 10 days.

Football, of course, was still football, and there was plenty to enjoy, and players to remember. Ted Eaglen, Ron Skidmore, Freddie Bett, Tiny Moore, Harry Sharpe, Sid Ottewell, Tommy Swinscoe and Ralph Robinson. And the usual arguments raged. Bert Trautmann, Footballer of the Year and the Manchester City goalkeeper, had suffered a broken his neck in the Cup Final following a collision with Birmingham's Peter Murphy. Should the charging of goalkeepers still be allowed? I thought not. Ought substitutes be allowed? I sat on the fence with that one, later climbing down in favour. There was even an increasing stroppiness among the crowds and a growing edge in the player and referee-baiting which had not been there before. One sensed the crowds were growing weary, and beginning to look for something new.

Meanwhile, things were still ticking over at the Valley. Frank Reed had taken over from Sam Bartram in goal - Sam was by now managing York City - and Townsend, Ufton, Ryan, White and Gauld had come into the side. At Carter's Park, I recall, there was a ripple of excitement when visitors Cambridge United named Wilf Mannion in their line-up for a league game against the Tigers. Wilf, the former England golden boy, had drifted from Middlesbrough and Hull to non-League Poole and then to Cambridge United, but in this game he struggled to make any real

*Holbeach United Colts, 1956. Back (left to right), Tommy Clay, Myland, Foreman, Hyde, Pite, Cooley, Bowers, Goodley, Len Richley; front, Tyler, Garrett, Keeble, Harris, Delahoy.*

impression. Against Randall, Yeardley, Watkins and Holbeach player-manager Len Richley he came up against an uncompromising defence, and a few shrewd, leisurely passes, most of which seemed to bemuse his fellow forwards as much as the opposition, did not in the end amount to much. Frankly, there was an element of sadness in the occasion, and the crowd sensed it. In any event, the Tigers won 1-0. But even they had other fish to fry. Long Sutton were drawn to play at Carter's Park in the Lincolnshire Senior Cup, which at least ensured that bus services between the two towns were kept busy.

*Holbeach United - Henry; Randall, Watkins; Tootill, Swallow, Richley; Hutchinson, Hurrell, Wilbert, Fox, Stamp.*

*Long Sutton Town - Anderson; Wells, Rumsey; Dye, Groom, Upson; Cain, Biggadike, McDonald, Willows, Button.*

In the autumn of 1956 I went to the Valley again and it was obvious that things were beginning to go seriously wrong. No Bartram, no Jimmy Seed for a start. After 18 matches Charlton had managed only three wins, they were languishing in last place in Division One, and worse, had been thrashed 8-1 by Sunderland, 4-0 by Leeds United, and 4-2 by Manchester United, who were leading the table from Tottenham and Blackpool. Recognising the crisis, manager Jimmy Trotter signed winger Sammy Lawrie and centre-forward Johnny Summers to bolster the scoring potential, but in the end it was to no avail. Charlton's world was crumbling, and they were on the verge of Division Two. The Valley was also beginning to show its age and the post-war 50,000-plus crowds had begun to sidle away.

I found it difficult to settle into work, and quickly discovered I had little or no interest in general news journalism. Finally, and perhaps recognising my increasing disenchantment, editor Sid Franks offered me the vacant post of Sports Editor of the Lincs Free Press and Spalding GuardianI accepted without a moment's thought. It did not save Charlton from the dreaded drop, but for me it was a shot in the arm.

*Charlton Athletic - Marsh; Hewie, Townsend; O'Linn, Ufton, Hammond; Lawrie, Ayre, Summers, Leary, Kinsey.*

*West Bromwich Albion - Sanders; Howe, Millard; Dudley, Kennedy, Barlow; Griffin, Robson, Kevan, Nicholls, Allen.*


If Wilf Mannion's presence at Carter's Park had set a few pulses momentarily racing, then there was the equivalent of an outbreak of mass hysteria in Spalding when the Tulips were drawn at the Halley Stewart playing field in an FA Cup qualifying round against Kettering Town. Not only were Kettering (the Poppies) a powerful and ambitious Midland League club, but more importantly, their attack was led by the great Tommy Lawton. The build-up to the game was wildly exciting, if not a little tense, for Spalding's regular 'keeper, Bramley, was not available and local youngster Peter Roberts was drafted in for what was dubbed the Battle of the Flowers. During the process of writing this I learned that Spalding's highest ever gate was 7000, achieved in the early 1950s when Peterborough United were entertained in an FA Cup-tie, but this, I think, was a shade before my time. On this day an excited match day crowd of 4100 poured across town to the park, forcing the kick-off to be delayed in order that everyone could get in.

Lawton, it must be said, was everything we imagined him to be. Lean, spring heeled and quick as a whippet, he always looked capable of scoring. He could certainly head a ball with the sort of conviction, power and direction I was not to see again until Norwich City signed Ron Davies (see Chapter 3). Tommy was also a great character, on and off the field, impish and unassuming, a centre-forward of the old school who knew instinctively that his role was to score goals and that no-one else could come remotely close to telling him how to do it. "Are you going to tell ME how to score goals?" he once asked quizzically of Walter Winterbottom when the England manager broached the subject of team tactics. Lawton knew nothing of tactics, nor saw the necessity. He was No 9, and he scored goals, and that was enough.

He had a point. For decades there had been a general inevitability about the way most sides played. Certainly before the war, and according to the evidence of filmed and written reports, including the 1930s feature film "The Arsenal Stadium Mystery," teams usually played with two wingers out wide, a lone No 9 backed by deep lying inside-forwards, and a defensive system which was invariably man-to-man rather than zonal. It was a game plan which allowed plenty of space for ball players to dwell on the ball and apply their art, and for forwards to flourish. Which the jut-jawed Lawton did, season after season.

As for the match, it was a thriller. Kettering were packed with players with League experience who knew how to counter-attack, Roberts made a series of extraordinary saves, and Spalding played out of their skins. After 20 minutes of non-stop action Prosser put Kettering ahead from Lawton's pass, only for Ron Jeffries to level 19 minutes later. Then in the 66th minute Megginson put the Tulips ahead for the first time while Jeffries, amid scenes of jubilation, made it 3-1 a few minutes later. Two minutes from time Lawton rose high over the home defence to head in a cross from the left. When the whistle went hundreds of blue and white adorned Spalding fans poured across the pitch to congratulate their heroes and to carry Roberts shoulder high to the dressing room.

Afterwards, I spoke to Tommy Lawton outside the Kettering changing room. He was courtesy itself, still grinning, his lean jaw still jutting defiantly. Yes, Spalding deserved their 3-2 win, he said. The goalie had played a grand game. Enjoyed the match enormously. Then he shook hands and he and the other Kettering players boarded their bus and slipped away into memory.

In a sense the occasion, performance and attendance represented a pinnacle of sorts. Never again was I able to sit in the Press box at the Halley Stewart, or on the Press bench at Carter's Park for that matter, to witness such a large local crowd enjoying such an exciting moment. From then on, and throughout the rest of my time with the Tulips and Tigers, it was downhill, economically speaking. The night Spalding celebrated victory over Kettering we did not know, nor would we have cared, that the framework of the game was changing, this time decisively, and that the structure of local football was already in decline.

*Spalding United - Roberts; Freeburn, Parker; Pickwick, R Robinson, Dennison; Birch, Megginson, Jeffries, Crouch, McCulloch.*
  *Kettering Town - Wheeler; McDonald, Jackson; Johnson, Plummer, Moss; Goodwin, Prosser, Lawton, Thomas, Robinson.*

The Tulips and the Tigers were as different as chalk and cheese. Whereas Spalding United were large and ambitious and run by accountants, estate agents and solicitors, Holbeach were compact and generally content, their affairs overseen by publicans and shopkeepers. This is not to decry one or the other, simply to point up the contrast. Whereas Spalding desperately wanted entry into the Midland League - they applied again in 1957 - Holbeach United rightly recognised it was out of their financial reach.

   Yet if nearby Peterborough United, with their posh new ground and undeniably fine team, were determined to achieve Football League status, then the Tulips could have their dreams, too. And they could do the business when it was needed. One murky autumn afternoon they beat Belper in the FA Cup and thus qualified for the first time to go into the hat for the first round proper with the Third Division clubs. This was the same Cup campaign, incidentally, which saw Wisbech beat Colchester United 1-0, Gorleston crash 10-1 at Gillingham, Norwich City trounce Redhill 6-1, and Peterborough United draw 3-3 with League side Torquay. As far as the Tulips were concerned the only dampener on this historic event was the actual draw itself. Durham City away.

   The area had not enjoyed a very great deal of success in the FA Cup. In the 1871-72 season, the very first that the Cup was played, Donington Grammar School for some reason entered a team and were rewarded with a bye. In the second round they were drawn away against Queen's Park, Glasgow; this time they failed to make the trip and Queen's Park were awarded a walkover. Most recent Cup efforts had been about as successful. But this one was different. This time Spalding stood a chance of getting among the big boys. The match also represented the first time I ever travelled away with a team, and I remember the journey well. We went by coach along the old A1 through Newark and stayed the night at Scotch Corner. Next morning it was on to Durham through an assorted collection of rainstorms, followed by a wet, misty welcome at City's homespun ground which seemed to have been hewn out of the side of a hill. Perhaps it was the rain or the quagmire pitch or the travelling, but the Tulips made precious little impact and lost 3-1.

   Nationally, at least, this was an expansive time for football. Manchester United, the first Football League club to enter the new European Cup,

reached the semi-final and then ran into Real
Madrid, losing in Spain and drawing 2-2 with
the Spanish masters at Old Trafford in front of a
61,000 crowd. And the great John Charles was
transferred from Leeds United to Juventus for
the then unheard of fee of £70,000. Perhaps there
was not much wrong with British football after
all?

*Freddie Fox*

Vic Cobley and David Bell at Spalding, and
Tommy Clay and Gordon Woodman at
Holbeach, among others, were determined to
keep the good times rolling even though there
was an increasing tendency to cast anxious eyes
at the attendances. Nevertheless, gates were still
high enough to provide a cash surplus. In the
days before the lid was taken off players' wages
League clubs invariably carried huge staffs.
Thus their A teams tended to be the equivalent
of today's Reserve teams, being made up of
three or four promising youngsters, three or four
hopefuls trying to get into the Reserve or First
team, and three or four experienced players
returning from injury or simply currently out

*Cyril Parrott*

of favour. Once the wages cap was removed, however, and when salary
bills climbed and gates started to decline, staff sizes were quickly pruned.
In consequence, there were plenty of ex-League players swilling around
the circuit hoping to extend their playing careers by a few more seasons
by picking up a little non-League cash.

Certainly at a local level there was great pressure on clubs to sign ex-
League players to placate the crowds. If your close rivals had them, then
you needed them, too. Anyway, they were glamorous, even though they
might only have got as far as Notts County Reserves. Even Holbeach, for
example, could afford to sign a goalkeeper, John Henry, from Tottenham
Hotspur. But there was a down side. The wall between the professional
and amateur games was being breached and would eventually fall, and,
because of a constant influx of experienced "outsiders," links with local
communities were becoming increasingly weakened and even broken.
Moreover, with a more "professional" attitude permeating the game local
football was losing its fluidity and, I suppose, its naivety. Things were
certainly changing, and the crowds were changing, too. For example,
Spalding might grumble at the paucity of a 1500 average gate, but they

could still point to over 16,300 members of the club's money-making pools ticket draw. Disaster was still some way off, but by the time serious financial problems did finally clutch at the hearts of many of the local clubs, much of the glamour had already evaporated and the crowds had gone.

A lot of this came back to me a season or two ago when Diss Town reached the non-League Cup Final at Wembley. In the 1950s the only route to Wembley for part-time professional clubs was through the FA Cup and thus at the end of a particularly long and difficult road, rendering it an impossible dream. Quite naturally, the effect on Diss and on the people of the surrounding area was extraordinary. And for a few days it was possible to glimpse, in Norfolk and north Suffolk, what it used to be like during the build-up to a South Lincolnshire local derby, Holbeach v Spalding.

At about this time, and with a certain nervous temerity, I applied on behalf of my weekly newspaper for a Press ticket to an FA Cup Final at Wembley. And got it. I remember the cavernous antiquity of the grand old stadium, the extraordinary crowds and colours and noise, the thrilling bravura of it all, the rickety platform leading to the Press box suspended high in the roof, the steaming mugs of hot Bovril, and the elite of Fleet Street, including some who evidently saw themselves as immortal and had thus assumed god-like characteristics. As for the game, it went off the boil when Villa left-winger Peter McParland clattered into Manchester United 'keeper Ray Wood in the 8th minute only for Wood to be carried off. Blanchflower, I seem to remember, took over in goal. McParland later scored twice - Taylor got a consolation goal for United - but despite a marvellous exhibition by Roger Byrne, in particular, the spectacle of the game was tarnished. And would you believe it, the Football Association still refused to move on the question of substitutes!

*Aston Villa - Sims; Lynn, Aldis; Crowther, Dugdale, Saward; Smith, Sewell, Myerscough, Dixon, McParland.*

*Manchester United - Wood; Foulkes, Byrne; Colman, Blanchflower, Edwards; Berry, Whelan, Taylor, Charlton, Pegg.*

The two local clubs' respective player-managers, Don Pickwick and Len Richley, were also as different as chalk and cheese. Whereas Spalding's Don Pickwick was an extrovert bundle of restless energy, Len, at Carter's Park, was taciturn and determined. Don turned out at right-half and played a chasing, harrying sort of game. In later years I was always reminded of him every time I saw Mal Lucas playing in a Norwich City shirt. In fact Don was an ex-Canary, a connection which enabled him to bring several former Norwich players to the Halley Stewart, including Ron Jeffries, who led the Tulips' attack with great subtlety for a number of seasons, winger Cliff Birch, and the impish Terry Ryder, who haunted penalty areas like a ghost and scored goal after unexpected goal at impossibly close ranges. He ended the 1957/58 season, for example, with 37 league goals and another 13 plundered in cup games. But Terry's stock was as changeable as the colour of a chameleon. One moment the crowds grew restless at his apparent lack of activity, or his lengthy "rest periods"; next minute they were cheering his latest goal to the skies. Don also ranged far and wide for his players and brought into the side such useful performers as Dennison, Harry and Ralph Robinson, that fine full-back Wally Freeburn (who with veteran Cyril Parrott comprised one of the safest full-back pairings in the region), and winger George Hair.

Len also had a knack of gathering good players some of whom, like locally-based Joe Price, were already at the club. I can recall Frankie Lynn and Gilbert, Brian Keeble, Graham Burrows, and the ebullient, ball-playing Freddie Fox. Richley also had to cope with the substantial gap left by the retirement of Ronnie Tootill. Ron had been the elegant midfield inspiration behind the Tigers' attack for some seven seasons, and he was sorely missed for a long time.

As a defensively minded left-half Richley, a fine organiser and a clever tactician, occasionally sallied upfield himself - it was known as "looking for a penalty" - when goals were in short supply. He was always trying things, changing formations, pushing players forward or wide or ordering them back, or introducing new dead ball routines. And he certainly had an eye for forwards. Brian Sharman was one, a goal poacher almost in the class of Terry Ryder, who hunted on the fringe of the penalty box. There was Eddie Dwane, a pacey left-winger, and enigmatic inside-forward Joe Hooley who, like Fox, had extraordinary ball control qualities. And then there was the exotic Nigerian international centre-forward Tesi "Thunder" Balogun, who I believe had a spell at Queen's Park Rangers.

Tesi, desperately anxious to establish himself in English football, was a tall, gangling athlete with a murderous shot - hence the nickname - and a degree of ball control that made most of the other players blush and crowds gasp in astonishment. At one stage, when it was known he was joining the Tigers, the story went round he would be playing in bare feet and that he had no need of boots. But I do not recall him ever doing so. One day I went to Boston to watch United play Peterborough United, then at the height of their non-League powers, and travelled back to Spalding with Tesi on the train. Sometime later he actually had a short spell with Boston, but at this stage he was leading the Tigers' line with sufficient dash to interest Colchester United manager Benny Fenton. During the train journey, it must be said, he was confident and cheerful and charming. But Tesi's game had a weakness which finally did for him as far as the British set-up was concerned. His game spluttered like fireworks, and he even had a spell in Holbeach Reserves. Had all the matches been played on the sort of surfaces that clay court tennis players use today, then he would have been king; but autumn and winter brought rain and snow, holding surfaces and mud-caked balls, and Tesi never did quite cope with the transition. He scored a lot of goals for Holbeach, and tried his luck at a number of clubs. Eventually, I believe, he returned to Nigeria.

*Boston United - King; Stafford, Snade; Hazeldine, Miller, Lowder; Hukin, Garvie, Graver, Lewis, Lister.*

*Peterborough United - Walls; Stafford, Chadwick; Shaw, Walker, Cranford; Hails, Emery, Donaldson, Longworth, McNamee.*


Match day sequences were invariably the same. For a Holbeach home game it would be a short journey to town on the bus followed by sandwiches and a cup of coffee, then a brief stroll down Park Road to Carter's Park, trying hard to avoid becoming embroiled in the banter of the fans as they streamed towards the entrance gates. "What bloody game were you at last week, then? It weren't the same game I saw." And so on. At the main ticket office beside the grandstand, open the door to the telephone stall and remove the security padlock from the dial. Obtain a programme, hammer on the visitors' dressing-room door and find someone to indicate the team changes. Then to the home dressing-room, exchange banter with the players, find Len for the Tigers' team changes and tell him who was in the opposition line-up. Give any changes from the printed programme to the match announcer who operated the Tannoy, then skirt the front of the grandstand to find the Press seat at the far end. More banter. "You don't know a good match from a bloody bad one." "Why do you write crap every week?" "You're a Spalding supporter - that's your trouble." But at least it was all reasonably friendly.

At Spalding it meant a walk across the Sheep Market and through Pied Calf Passage, not far from where the old British Restaurant used to be. Then I would join the crowds funnelling towards the Halley Stewart ground and endure basically the same jokes. "Didn't recognise the match you wrote about last week." "You're a Holbeach supporter, that's your trouble." Again, jokey and friendly rather than aggressive. Walk along the touchline to the old wooden Press box; unlock the door, unlock the phones (sometimes a visiting reporter would arrive, needing a phone to

*A youthful Bruce Robinson watches as Tulips' player-manager Don Pickwick (left) welcomes amateur international goalkeeper Mike Pinner (right) to the club.*

send match copy to his Saturday Pink Un, or whatever); then go outside and unfasten the wooden front shutter, which lifted from the bottom and was propped up by iron stanchions. Usual chaff from youngsters sitting on the grass between the Press box and the touchline. "Sell us a paper, mister." "Got any ice cream?" A Spalding official would arrive with a programme and the team changes, and again mid-way through the second half with the attendance. It was a splendid service, but we always believed it was a ruse to keep us away from the dressing-rooms.

For the most part it was good fun even though the football was deadly serious. These were the days when Elvis Presley and Bill Haley blared out from the loudspeakers of nearby funfairs, of Sputnik, and Bernstein's "West Side Story," of bubble cars and scooters, of Brazil (Vava, Garrincha, Zagallo, Pele, Bellini, Djalma, Nilton, Didi, etc) sweeping Sweden aside 5-2 in the

World Cup Final and thus hoisting the game to new artistic and technical levels, and of Bolton beating Manchester United 2-0 in the FA Cup Final after poor Gregg, the United 'keeper, was injured early on in a clash with Lofthouse.

Locally, there was much to enjoy, too, including that fine forward Ronnie Codd at Spalding, along with Mulholland and Ron Hewitt; while Holbeach had the young and hugely talented Ray Garrett, Gordon Pateman, Ray Swallow, and Brian Stamp, the Tigers' irrepressible left-winger.

*Spalding United - Hewitt; Freeburn, Parrott; Williams, Flowers, Dennison; Mulholland, Ryder, Jeffries, Codd, Hair.*

*Chelmsford Reserves - Evans; Brewer, Baldwin; CArter, Farley, Gardiner; Page, Sinnott, Mingay, Tuttlebury, Brennan.*

One day in February, needing a break from subbing sports copy, I wandered into the Free Press reporters' room to scrounge a cigarette. Someone had just taken a telephone call and had made an announcement, and they were all sitting there white-faced and silent.

"What's up?"

"The Manchester United plane has crashed at Munich. A lot of them are dead."

It was scarcely believable, though alas true. Some exceptionally fine players were lost that day including Duncan Edwards, Mark Jones, Bill Whelan, Roger Byrne, David Pegg, Eddie Colman, Tommy Taylor and Geoff Bent. Press men too, such as former England 'keeper Frank Swift, Archie Ledbrook (Daily Mirror), Henry Rose (Daily Express) and Tom Jackson (Manchester Evening News). In later years I used to wonder how many of that lost playing squad would have found their way into the England World Cup winning formation of 1966. Duncan Edwards, almost certainly; probably Roger Byrne and possibly Eddie Colman. Perhaps more. The loss was immense, and everyone knew it.

*Manchester United (assorted squad from the late 1950s) - Wood, Edwards, Taylor, Whelan, Bent, Foulkes, Blanchflower, Webster, McGuinness, Viollet, Colman, Berry, Jones, Byrne, Pegg, Charlton.*

There were several attempts to reorganise the local leagues, for it was clear the game had entered a period of decisive change, and divisions, zones, mergers and take-overs entered the local soccer vocabulary as the ECL and Midland Leagues, together with the United Counties League and even the Lincolnshire and Spalding and District Leagues, jostled and talked, argued and manoeuvred. Some of the League club A teams (Spurs, Lincoln City, for example) were still around, but it was clear they were being pulled in other directions. Instead, there were new names on the Spalding and Holbeach fixture lists: Symingtons, Phorbes Sports, Rushden, Wellingborough, Desborough, Appleby Frodingham, Louth, Lincoln Claytons, Lysaghts and Barton Town.

Round about the time that Len Richley celebrated the third extension of his contact at Holbeach it became plain, particularly at Spalding, that a financial crisis was looming. Membership of the Tulips' fund-raising pool was dropping alarmingly and gates were falling. It seemed to me that the Tulips, particularly, were ignoring the warning signs as though they were a blip in the accounts. I started a campaign in the Spalding Guardian arguing that expenditure, and particularly expenditure on visiting part-time professional players, should be cut back and the talents of more local players utilised instead. The deterioration was surprisingly rapid. By the end of 1958 the Holbeach gate was down to an average of 600 while Spalding's had collapsed to between 700 and 1200, depending on opposition. At one Spalding annual meeting it was revealed the club had an annual wages bill of £1000 and that only four of the club's players were amateurs.

Then we came into direct conflict. Because of my published views about the future of football, and local football finances, Spalding United decided they would no longer make a copy of the balance sheet available to the Free Press or the Guardian, or allow entry into the annual meeting. I went to see editor Sid Franks.

"I've got a problem. The Tulips won't let me have a copy of the balance sheet."

"Who do they send balance sheets to?"

"Shareholders."

"Then buy some shares," he said.

So I did. Two. As a matter of fact I still have the certificate, now quite worthless and relegated to the role of souvenir. Share certificate 126, two shares at five shillings each, dated September 8, 1958. The fly in the ointment was that Sid would not allow me to claim the ten shillings back through expenses.

On February 6, 1959, and after a lot of hard work, the Spalding Guardian published a full page broadsheet survey of the state of Eastern Counties League football, for I wanted to see how Holbeach and Spalding were faring in relation to the rest of the clubs. My survey was headlined: "They're All In The Cart - In One Way Or Another."

Some of the figures are worth repeating. Of the clubs who replied to my request for information, and in the matter of players' wages, Spalding emerged as the biggest spenders of the lot with an annual bill of £5250. Holbeach's wages bill, including expenses, amounted to £4500. Lowestoft, in fifth place, spent £1700 on players' wages, while at Gorleston the bill was a mere £700. These levels of expenditure were also reflected in the playing staffs. Spalding, for example, had 21 full or part-time professional players (only 10 of whom lived within 20 miles of the Halley Stewart) and no amateurs in their senior squad. Holbeach had 20 full or part-timers and four amateurs. All eleven of Yarmouth's regular first teamers were amateur players, while Gorleston had five professionals and six amateurs. As for attendances, they were all in decline. Lowestoft had an average of 1563, the league's highest; Spalding's average had dropped to 1177 while Holbeach were struggling by on 350. I concluded: "Football is dying with its boots on. Professionalism, born and bred in local circles in an era of white hot enthusiasm after the war, is beginning to defeat its own purpose."

Some sectors of non-League football, however, were still doing rather well. At Peterborough, for example. While at Wisbech manager Oscar Hold had gathered together one of the most impressive of all the local formations, including England B international Johnny Crosland, England caps Jesse Pye, Billy Elliott and Bobby Langton, and former Manchester United inside-forward Johnny Downie. If that was impressive, so were some of the Fenmen's gates, which in the Midland League averaged about 2000. Once, when Wisbech played Peterborough United, the attendance topped 8000.

When the Tulips met Tottenham A at Cheshunt in a mid-week away fixture I travelled with them and had the good fortune to meet Maurice Withers, then coaching the Spurs' side, and Monty Norman, who at been at Carrow Road with Don Pickwick. It was a cause of satisfaction at the time to reflect that such fine Spurs' players as Dodge, Laurel, White, Hollowbread, Dunmore and Duquemin had all played at Carter's Park at one time or another, and probably at the Halley Stewart, too.

Later that year Boston United entertained French side Laval, with whom the town was twinned, in a floodlit friendly match. It was a curious, edgy encounter and one that brought into focus the different approaches to the game which had developed on either side of the Channel. British tackling techniques left the French amateurs bemused and bruised, the referee's decisions were often a source of puzzlement, and even though Boston had agreed for the sake of cross-Channel friendship to a rule that goalkeepers should not be charged, the surprised French custodian was sent flying on at least one occasion.

*Boston United - King; Adams, Stafford; Cleary, Sims, Clarke; Graver, Cresswell, King, Neale, Barnes.*

*Laval - Pillon; Calvez, Postec; Douguet, Miko, Chassard; Garry, Gaumer, Leguy, Boisseau, Mauduit.*

THURSDAY, 16th OCTOBER, 1958.
**Boston United** v. **LAVAL** (FRANCE)
KICK-OFF 7.00 P.M.

Occasionally you came across someone who added something to the match entertainment. In addition to the regulation brass band, that is. One such visitor was Norwich referee Tommy Dawes who regularly officiated at local grounds before being elevated to the League list, one of his early jobs being a Cup-tie between Aston Villa and Burnley. Tommy brought originality on to the pitch in that he invariably explained his decisions to the players, he always smiled, and he had a knack of being able to de-fuse potentially difficult moments. In Holbeach and Spalding he

*Programme for the Boston United versus Laval match, 1958.*

was known as the "laughing ref," and one moment I particularly savour occurred at Spalding when he stopped a match after two illegal throw-ins and demonstrated to the embarrassed players exactly how a throw should be taken.

Another Norfolk connection also dominated the headlines at the time - Norwich City, and their spectacular success in the FA Cup and ultimate defeat in the semi-final. I did not see any of those matches, but I did fill a Press seat at the subsequent Wembley Cup Final. It was yet another game badly affected by injury, this time to Nottingham Forest winger Dwight who had to leave the pitch after half an hour. Forest eventually won, but the spectacle of ten men against 11, once thought of as heroic, was becoming as regular an event as the debate over substitutes.

*Nottingham Forest - Thomson; Whare, McDonald; Whitefoot, McKinley, Burkitt; Dwight, Quigley, Wilson, Gray, Imlach.*

*Luton Town - Baynham; McNally, Hawkes; Groves, Owen, Pacey; Bingham, Brown, Morton, Cummins, Gregory.*


At about the time that the threat of a provincial Press strike began to hover in the air I applied for a vacancy on the sports staff of the Eastern Evening News in Norwich, and subsequently got the job. It was a time of enormous change not only for myself but for a lot of people. Peterborough United were on the verge of election to the Football League, Brian Keeble had left the Tigers to sign for Second Division Grimsby Town, Long Sutton Town announced their average gate was "practically nil," and Len Richley and Don Pickwick revealed their intentions to try pastures new. In Len's case this was the managership of King's Lynn FC. It was also the end of my weekly Football Column which had run for two seasons and nearly 80 editions of the Spalding Guardian.

Len, I believe, left Holbeach relatively quietly, having done a marvellous job and having put his name in the club's record books alongside those of Jock Basford, Archie Garrett and Bruce Ward. Being factual about it, he left them highly placed in the ECL with £9000 in the bank and one of the best youth sides in the county. This in a town of 7000 people. Don's departure was somewhat noisier and considerably more public, for in April, 1959, he persuaded Norwich City to visit the Halley Stewart for his benefit match, only a few months after their FA Cup exploits had pushed them into the national headlines. Don (who was subsequently replaced by Sid Ottewell), Terry Ryder and Ron Jeffries, ex-Canaries themselves, knew most of the visitors, while I was meeting a Norwich City team for the first time. And most of the Cup side were there, only Bryan Thurlow and Jimmy Hill being missing. An excited Spalding crowd of over 2700 saw City win 4-1.

*Spalding United - Woolgar; Fidler, Parrott; Pickwick, Robinson, Williams; Codd, Smith, Jeffries, Hair, Rackham.*

*Norwich City - Nethercott; Mullett, Ashman; McCrohan, Butler, Crowe; Crossan, Allcock, Bly, Moran, Brennan.*


Some weeks after this match I, like Don and Len, also departed. Before I went the Tigers' new manager, Henry Dove, let me write a few "farewell" paragraphs for the match programme. They were duly published when Holbeach United entertained Spalding United in an Eastern Counties League match on September 2, 1959, the first South Lincolnshire derby I had missed for several years. For some reason I penned a brief and somewhat soppy plea for local players to be given a better crack of the whip. I have no recollection now of who won the game, but I do remember it as an extremely difficult break to make.

*Holbeach United - Egglestone; Swallow, Randall; Price, Dove, Watkins; Adams, Clark, Hutchinson, Hooley, Lynn.*

*Spalding United - Woolgar; Fidler, Rushworth; Collins, Robinson, Lord; Paul, Cluroe, Jeffries, Ryder, Middlemass.*

*A Spalding United programme of 1958.*

# 3 Second Half
# 1959-1973

▬ ▬ ▬ ▬ ▬ ▬ ▬ ▬

Norwich in 1959, rather like Spalding, was still in the process of shedding the conventions and restrictions of the war years. It had only just begun to flex its commercial and social muscles, and was feeling its way cautiously. The Canaries' Cup run of 1958/59, which came to a harrowing end against Luton Town in the semi-final, had bathed the region in a new light of hope; they were still talking about it on a, "Phew, you should have seen it!" basis. But some things had not changed. Archie Macaulay was still in the manager's chair and Harry Banger was still producing his Canary and Dump cartoons for the Pink Un. Eating places were few and austere, for the first Chinese restaurant had not then arrived. The remnants of a once busy Cattle Market still lingered, but the only swimming pool was in the open air at Lakenham. Nevertheless, the city did have three huge stadia in addition to Carrow Road. These were the Firs speedway stadium, which had terraces and a grandstand and which could hold crowds of 20,000; the City greyhound racing stadium near the Sprowston road roundabout; and Boundary Park dog track, where there were also terraces and grandstands and where Norwich City A team played. Cinemas like the Theatre Royal, the Regal and the Hippodrome, were gloomy, drafty places, often sparsely populated, and nose to tail two-way traffic inched its way through London Street, forcing pedestrians to flatten themselves against shop fronts to avoid being crushed. At the Norfolk News Company, then housed in a honeycomb of offices hidden behind a sparkling new façade in Redwell Street, Ted Bell had overall charge as Sports Editor, while David Dunn covered the City matches for the Eastern Evening News and Danny Marks (White Line) for the Eastern Daily Press. I spent most of the day disinterestedly subbing racecards for the evening paper.

The system then in operation in the sports department meant that almost everyone on the day shift, particularly the newcomer, was also given

Saturday and evening jobs. I found myself covering hockey, lawn tennis and athletics, and spending most Saturday nights at the speedway, for Ove Fundin and the Stars were still drawing up to 7000 fans to the Firs. It was exciting at first, but Fundin began to win everything, the sport became tedious, and a desperation move to introduce a handicapping system failed to capture the public imagination. Eventually the Firs was sold for housing. City Stadium went the same way, while Boundary Park - after some discussion as to whether Norwich City ought to move there - finally came into the possession of the Electricity Board. Within a surprisingly very few years the city would be bemoaning the lack of a decent stadium, essentially for athletics, glossing over the fact that it had allowed three to disappear.

Ted also started me writing a weekly sports column in the EN, much of it, I note, about football. There were also numerous articles about the problems of many of the local soccer clubs, particularly those on the Norfolk coast. One of the general difficulties was that gates were falling as more and more people either stayed in and watched television, trooped down to Carrow Road, or went for a drive in their new car. Another was that the ECL, a regional competition spread from Tottenham and Chelmsford to Spalding and Lowestoft, required that local clubs meet an enormous travelling bill. By the end of 1959 many of them were in dire trouble. Yarmouth (manager, Eric Lewis), £1400 in debt in 1958 and facing eviction from the Wellesley, had seen their support shrink from an average of 2000 to about 490. They needed 800 a game simply to pay the bills, they told me. Lowestoft (team captain Don Pickwick, fresh from Spalding) had painstakingly built up a useful amateur side only to lose many of their players to part-time professional clubs; had turned professional themselves when gates were about 1500, and had promptly seen them sink to about 800. As for Gorleston, (coach, ex-Charlton player Bert "Sailor" Brown), they were 16th in the league, forecasting the end of their foray into semi-professionalism, and struggling to survive on crowds of 300. Once, 9000 packed the Recreation Ground.

Occasionally I was also dragooned into covering those matches at Carrow Road, often midweek night games, which no-one else wanted to attend. One of them was an FA X1 v the Royal Air Force, who turned out a side made up of players from Accrington Stanley, Coventry, Cardiff and Colchester United, but who also had Macleod of Hibs and big Jim Clunie of Aberdeen in their ranks. In the event the the FA won a leisurely canter 9-2 with a side which included City's Bryan Thurlow and Terry Bly, and well-known players such as Gordon Milne, Peter Swan, winger John Connelly, Fred Hill and Jimmy Melia.

*FA X1 - Humphries; Thurlow, Ashurst; Milne, Swan, Smith; Connelly, F Hill,*
*Bly, Melia, Sydenham.*
  *RAF - Brown; McNeice, Raine; Stones, Clunie, Curtis; McMillan, Webb, King,*
*Fulton, Macleod.*


One place where gates were holding up was at Carrow Road, for there
was still a feeling of heady expectation after the previous season's Cup
run. Attendances of 30,000 (or 36,000 when Barnsley were the visitors)
were by no means rare, particularly as the side settled into contention for
promotion from the old Third Division South. This was still Norwich
football in the grand manner, full of sweeping attacking movements, and
it was a pleasure to stand on a Wednesday night with the rest of the packed
Barclay Enders' fraternity to watch Ashman, Crowe and Butler short-pass
their way out of defensive trouble, or Crossan and Allcock tear chunks
out of a visiting defence.
  Opportunities for actually covering soccer matches were limited, but I
did manage to visit Filbert Street, purely for my own pleasure, to see
Leicester take on Sheffield Wednesday. Leicester, under Matt Gillies, had
lost their way a little, and even though they had Gordon Banks in goal
and Appleton and Knapp to bolster the defence they were dangerously
close to the relegation zone. As for Wednesday, Tom McAnearney was
still there and Ron Springett was in goal, but Froggatt and Fantham had
taken over from Quixall and Sewell, and the side had been largely reshaped
since I had last seen them.
  Shortly before Christmas referee Tommy Dawes, then living in Thorpe,
reappeared on the scene. Tommy was now on the League list and officiating
at League games on a regular basis, but when I caught up with him again
he was preparing to referee CNS Old Boys versus CEYMS at Britannia
Barracks. The previous Saturday it had been Brighton v Sunderland in
Division Two. A comedown? Not a bit, said Tommy. Enjoy it. In fact he
went on to say that on days off from League duty he also helped to look
after Norfolk and Suffolk League and Business Houses League matches.
Even when he got mud in his whistle he was still smiling.
  A few days before Christmas, 1959, an office inevitability duly occurred.
Pre-festivity gloom because the Canaries had a Boxing Day fixture at
Mansfield and none of the regular writers wanted to go. Other things to
do. Families, and all that. Ted asked me nicely: would I mind? So on the
morning of the match, armed with a flask of soup and surrounded by
flurries of snow, I drove to Field Mill. This was the first occasion I reported
a League match, but there was no glory to describe. City were 3-0 down

after 76 minutes, thanks to the marvellous Lindy Delaphena, one of the few players to properly master the mud; and despite a late rally, they lost 3-2. It seemed a very long drive home.

Inevitably, there was an embarrassing moment during my League Press box debut. It was the practice in those days, if the first team was playing away and there was a Reserve match at Carrow Road, to let the ground know the score at regular intervals so that it could be announced over the loudspeakers. Carrow Road booked calls to the away Press box every 20 minutes or so. When a call came through in about the 80th minute I picked up the phone and passed on the gloomy news that City were trailing 3-0. Then I glimpsed Hill sliding the ball into the

*Archie Macaulay*

home net. "It's 3-1. Jimmy Hill's just scored," I said, replacing the receiver, pleased with the lateness of this late news. Then I saw the referee had whistled for off-side and that the goal was disallowed. Hastily, I called Carrow Road. "I've made a mistake. The goal was disallowed." But it was too late; the news had been broadcast to the fans. Two minutes later Hill did indeed score to make it 3-1. "You lucky beggar," said club secretary Bert Westwood, when I phoned again to give him the glad tidings. The crowd at the reserve match that day never knew they received news of a City goal two minutes before it was scored.

*Mansfield - Wyllie; Humble, Bradley; Williams, Ripley, Jayes; Ringstead, Delaphena, Jones, Fitzsimmons, Hall.*

*Norwich City - Kennon; Thurlow, Ashman; McCrohan, Butler, Crowe; Crossan, Allcock, Bly, Hill, Punton.*

As the City challenge for promotion gathered pace and local attendances stayed at around the 30,000 mark, it was two foreign teams who actually dominated the national newspaper headlines - Eintracht Frankfurt, and more particularly, Real Madrid. Their European Cup final match at Hampden Park had been watched by an enormous 127,000 crowd who had paid between 5s and 50s for the privilege. It was even shown on BBC TV complete with commentary by Kenneth Wolstenhome. The encounter created great comment and excitement, for Real's style of play was as different from the British game as chalk from cheese; the Daily Mail headline on Don Hardisty's match report read, bluntly - "Soccer as She is Played."

I was not at Hampden Park, of course, but a year or two ago I did purchase a BBC video of the game, minus the four minutes lost because of a Glasgow power cut. Looking at it again 35 years after the actual event it is easy to understand why soccer enthusiasts have retained such a warm feeling for the encounter, why it has stuck in the memory. First, most of the Real players were held in considerable awe by British fans (the skills of Gento and Di Stefano were legendary, and the part played by the great Hungarian, Puskas, in the demolition of England a few years before had not been forgotten), and there were no smothering defences, packed midfields or tackles from the back. Instead, those lucky enough to be at Hampden on the night - and the BBC, alas, gave only fleeting glimpses of the huge terraces - witnessed an open, end-to-end, elegant, free-flowing encounter. The stuff of dreams, perhaps, and a match you could not afford to tear your eyes away from, for there was no after-match analysis or endless action replays. Blink, and you missed a goal. Anyway, it is enough to record that on that cold Glasgow night Puskas scored four and Di Stefano three, the crowd went home warm and happy, and that the two teams were: Eintracht - Loy; Lutz, Heofer, Weilbocher, Eigenbrodt, Stinka, Kress, Lindner, Stein, Pfaff, Meier. Real Madrid - Dominquez; Marquitos, Pachin, Vidal, Santamaria, Zarraga, Canario, Del Sol, Di Stefano, Puskas, Gento.

Meanwhile, the Canaries duly gained long-awaited promotion to Division Two, though the FA Cup bubble burst decisively at Reading and there were to be no serious dreams of Wembley for several more years. Knowing that the old order was changing and that reinforcements were necessary, Archie Macaulay, never one to give much away, suddenly and unexpectedly popped up with two signings, Brian Whitehouse from WBA and Bunny Larkin from Birmingham. Archie had always kept everyone guessing, specially Pressmen, making sure his powder was constantly dry. Despatched to Carrow Road during earlier pre-season training to write a piece for the EEN, I had asked Archie about the possibility of signings. "We have no new faces this morning," he retorted cagily. It meant everything and nothing. However, when Charlton visited Carrow Road on a Wednesday evening for the second fixture of the season only Bunny Larkin of the two made the starting line-up.

*Norwich City - Kennon; Thurlow, Ashman; McCrohan, Butler, Crowe; Crossan, Hill, Allcock, Larkin, Punton.*
*Charlton Athletic - Duff; Sewell, Townsend; Hinton, Jago, Lucas; Lawrie, White, Summers, Werge, Kiernan.*

Lower down the scale the fourth annual meeting of the Norwich Sunday League admitted another 16 clubs, taking the total to 36, bluntly underlining that Sunday football was there to stay and that the structure demanded, and eventually achieved, parity with the Saturday game in terms of administration and refereeing. Nationally, many of the big League clubs were still being decidedly sniffy about the new fangled League Cup complaining with some justification, as indeed some of them still do, that they already played too many matches. There was no mistaking the fact that it was a time of change. Norwich City programmes still referred to shorts as knickers, the main grandstand and Press box were timber-built and facilities in the dank and dismal interior of the ground were minimal. But City were in Division Two, and Peterborough United were finally admitted to the League under the managership of Jimmy Hagan, the former Sheffield United wizard.

The Canaries, however, did embrace the ethos of the League Cup, arguing logically that it doubled their chances of Cup, if not Wembley, glory and brought in extra revenue. It also brought fresh faces to Carrow Road, as if the Second Division clubs were not new enough; but I do not think even the most fervent of fans would have anticipated City's 4-1 League Cup victory on a bitterly cold and wet Monday night on a quagmire pitch at Derby's Baseball Ground. It was also interesting because City's line-up that night still featured the famed defence of the Cup-run days, but an entirely new attack. Anyway, I presume no-one else from the office wanted to go. In the end I quite enjoyed the occasion, phoning my first full-length match report through to the Eastern Daily Press.

The Canaries, of course, went on next season to lift the League Cup, winning a two-leg damp squib final tie against Rochdale. It illustrated precisely why the League management committee was forced to bring Wembley Stadium into the formula, to give the competition a bit of stature, the fans something to dream about, and more importantly, to win the approval of the big boys.

*Derby County - Adlington; Barrowcliffe, Conwell; Parry, Smith, Upton; Swallow, Hall, Curry, Hutchinson, Fagan.*
*Norwich City - Kennon; Thurlow, Ashman; McCrohan, Butler, Crowe; Spelman, Lythgoe, Whitehouse, Larkin, Punton.*

Changes to the game even deeper than arguments over the League Cup were also taking place, one of them relating to the continued division between the amateur and the professional games. Tales of banknotes in amateur players' boots were rife; and true or not, there is little doubt that the edges of the two games were becoming blurred. This problem was not solely confined to football, of course. Rugby had divided many years earlier, resulting in the creation of two codes, but soccer's problems were not of this order. Great Britain, for example, was still sending football sides to the Olympic Games, despite the fact that it was becoming increasingly difficult to distinguish between the two sets of players. Who were amateur and who were professional? Were there any amateur players left? In the end it all became too much, and a tradition died. An Olympic tradition died, too, for there seemed little prospect then, or now for that matter, that home country FAs would ever become sufficiently close to organise a professional Great Britain squad, a basic requirement for entry to the Games. Other sports also abandoned the differentiation, eventually. Racing, you may recall, had that awful business where amateur riders were known as Mr Bloggs whereas professional riders were known, simply and bluntly, as Bloggs. As for cricket, it had Gentlemen v Players and scorecards cluttered with strings of initials - or not, as the case may be - simply to reinforce a supposed difference in playing status.

Aside from the pro/amateur debate, money was also at the top of the full-time League players' agenda. George Eastham, then a Newcastle United player, wanted to leave to join Arsenal, but the Magpies would not let him go. He took them to court. The episode mushroomed into a players' challenge by the Professional Footballers' Association ably led, it must be said, by former Fulham forward and later television pundit Jimmy Hill, on the varied questions of money, contracts and the maximum wage, which then stood at £20 a week. A strike was threatened and in the end a deal was cobbled together. It was the "end of slavery," the players said. From then on they could negotiate their own wages and conditions, something club boards had not had to deal with before.

But the amateur game lingered. In January, 1961, the same month as the PFA and the League reached agreement, Bungay Town were drawn away to Leytonstone in an FA Amateur Cup first round replay. I went with them. Heavy rain during the morning so alarmed the home club they called in the referee to inspect the pitch, but eventually he gave it the go-ahead even though "puddles of water covered the touchlines, most of the rest of the pitch was quickly churned into a bog of rich, melted chocolate-coloured mud, and the white lines around the centre circle disappeared." More, they all trooped off the field "looking like an advertisement for the 'Black and White Minstrel Show.'" Bungay need not have bothered. Nearly 1500 partisan home fans saw Leytonstone win 5-0.

*Leytonstone - Griffin; Allen, Wood; Smith, Newman, Messer; Hammond, Day, Greenhill, Tiffin, Hill.*

*Bungay Town - Moore; Fairhead, High; Raven, Collins, Hamond; Fisher, Ludbrook, Green, Beck, Yallop.*

There were compensations, however. In April, England walloped Scotland 9-3 with what Alan Hoby (Sunday Express) said was the finest England attack he had ever seen. For the record it read: Douglas, Greaves, Smith, Haynes and Charlton. Two months later, and shortly before Tottenham beat Leicester City 2-0 at Wembley to complete the first League and Cup double by any club since 1897, I was ordered to Wembley for a Wednesday night game to get something of the feel of an international occasion.

England's opponents were Mexico, who had won 2-1 when the two sides met at altitude in Mexico City in 1959. Walter Winterbottom certainly did not under-rate the visitors, whose counter-attacking game had unsettled Holland in Amsterdam and who had some fine individual players, particularly goalkeeper Antonio Carvajal, winger Del Aguila and "Panchito" Flores, a marvellous mid-field player. Nevertheless, England looked comfortable in their 4-2-4 framework, with Bobby Robson and Johnny Haynes in mid-field, and there were 77,000 at the statium to cheer them on. No Jimmy Greaves, Johnny Byrne (the first Fourth Division player to turn out for England) or Bobby Smith, but Gerry Hitchens (Aston Villa) leading the attack with the ubiquitous Derek Kevan (WBA), a much argued over player, at inside-right. Kevan, who patently lacked pace at this level, became the unfortunate player most fans loved to dislike. Mexico, if memory serves me, more or less played three at the back, two in the middle and five in attack.

In the end Winterbottom, and Kevan, need not have worried too much. Minutes before the kick-off Mexico for some reason switched their goalkeeper, bringing in the diminutive Mota for Carvajal. Kevan scored the opening goal and England won at a canter 8-0. Mexico were swamped.

*England - Springett; Armfield, Swan, Flowers, McNeil; Robson, Haynes; Douglas, Kevan, Hitchens, Charlton.*

*Mexico - Mota; Pena, Jauregui, Cardenas; Sepulveda, Portugal; Del Aguila, Reyes, Gonzales, Flores, Mercado.*

Norwich City's introduction to life in Division Two looked promising enough. They held their own and a stream of new players arrived, including that erratic yet talented winger George Waites (Leyton Orient), Jim Conway, a tireless striker from Celtic, Gerry Mannion (Wolves), who could play wide on either flank, and Ollie Burton, a classy wing-half from from Newport County. Carrow Road also saw some 40,000-plus attendances when Sunderland and Ipswich came in the FA Cup. But somehow the glow had dimmed; Cup glory eluded them, and it was plain Division Two would be no pushover. Despite the injection of new faces and new clubs on the fixture list, City were beginning to look a tad ordinary, which is the worst of worlds for the enthusiastic supporter. Then in October, 1961, Archie Macaulay resigned and joined WBA at the Hawthorns.

During the interregnum Peterborough United, by then in the Third Division, visited Carrow Road for a friendly match (United - Walls; Whittaker, Hawkes; Rayner, Walker, Ripley; Hails, Emery, Bly, Hudson, McNamee), and shortly afterwards the City board unveiled their surprise choice as manager, Willie Reid, previously with St Mirren. Willie was an unknown quantity as far as the English League and the City fans were concerned, and all in all it was a somewhat curious interlude. Curiouser still was the fact that he eventually resigned after only a few months, apparently leaving Norwich "on friendly terms." One wag suggested the parting came about because Reid could not understand the Norfolk dialect while the players could not interpret his broad Scots' accent. True or not, it left another managerial vaccum at Carrow Road and put chairman Geoffrey Watling back in his "caretaker" role.

In later years, when I was the EDP's regular soccer writer, Geoffrey occasionally found himself in this position. It was a role he relished, although there was always tremendous pressure for the board to fill the vacancy as soon as possible. Geoffrey Watling's long association with the club was forged in the 1950s when the club was facing financial ruin. Chairmen, even as late as the 1960s, tended to be background boys who kept things ticking over, kept an eye on the administration, and only really emerged into the sunlight of the public gaze at a time of crisis or when hiring and firing a manager. Certainly they took more of a back seat than now. It was as though there was some sort of tacit understanding that football, and the manager, were the public face of the club, and that the directors simply held the assets and good name of the club in trust.

At times such as these, however, when the club was between manager or there was some sort of crisis of confidence or cash, we the Press would walk from our Redwell Street offices to Tombland to be ushered into the presence of the chairman in his upstairs office overlooking the cathedral gates. I must say he was helpfulness personified. If he felt under pressure, from us or the fans, he would explain the position of the board as simply as he could and field our questions as cleanly and clearly as he could. He left the indelible impression that he was a pair of safe hands and that the club would come to no harm while it was within his domain. I think it was the stability he engendered that laid the foundation of the Canaries' later successes.

*Norwich City - Barnsley; McCrohan, Ashman; Scott, Butler, Crowe; Mannion, Allcock, Conway, Hill, Lythgoe.*

*Charlton Athletic - Duff; Sewell, Hewie; Tocknell, Hinton, Bailey; Lawrie, Matthews, Leary, Edwards, Kinsey.*

In May, 1962, Geoffrey Watling unveiled the next Norwich City manager. There had been intense speculation for a fortnight before his name was revealed, but there was a strong clue the previous weekend when a posh car with an unusual registration number was spotted by the EDP in the Carrow Road car park. It read: AFC 100. The man in question was George Swindin, the former Arsenal manager and the Gunners' goalkeeper for 18 years. I was there the day he took over. George made it plain he was a disciplinarian and a tracksuit manager, that he was going to play 4-2-4, like most other sides, and that he saw football as an entertainment. "What the public want to see is goals," he told me, adding that his duties related solely to football matters and that he would have no truck with administration. It was a significant separation of jobs.

Alas, I did not see City on a regular basis, but I did manage to visit Wembley (a midweek afternoon kick-off) see watch England, with Greaves, John Connelly and Ray Wilson in the side, win 3-1 against a useful Switzerland side made up of full and part-time professionals, among them a building contractor, a commercial traveller, a decorator and a bank cashier. A few weeks later there was a chance to see Alf Ramsey's buoyant Ipswich outfit in a Division One fixture against top of the table Wolves.

*Ipswich Town - Bailey; Malcolm, Compton; Baxter, Nelson, Elsworthy; Stephenson, Moran, Crawford, Phillips, Blackwood.*

*Wolverhampton Wanderers - Davies; Showell, Thomson; Goodwin, Woodfield, Flowers; Wharton, Crowe, McParland, Murray, Hinton.*

These were unnerving times for City supporters, for a third managerial change in less than a year was hardly the sort of continuity they were seeking. Yet even they recognised the side needed a fairly major over-haul. Certainly George Swindin did. The Cup glory days had gone, the euphoria of promotion dissipated, and the squad needed to adapt to cope with the rigours of Division Two. Swindin entered the fray with a will, spending over £50,000, a sum of money large enough to have impressed anyone and to have announced to the world (ground admission prices were then anywhere between 1s 6d and 10s 6d) that this was a Club with Ambition. Into the ranks came winger Alistair Miller, from St Mirren, defender Barry Staton (Doncaster), wing-half Jackie Bell from Newcastle, Jim Oliver from Falkirk, right-back Phil Kelly from Wolverhampton Wanderers and forward Gareth Salisbury from Wrexham. He even tried to prise Stuart Leary from Charlton. But in possibly the most significant signing of them all, he made use of the Willie Reid connection by going back to St Mirren for Tommy Bryceland, a skilful and influencial inside-forward of the old school who was to have a profound effect on the Canaries' future over the next eight seasons.

Some of City's Cup squad were still there: Ashman, Allcock, Butler, Hill, Kennon, McCrohan and Thurlow, for example, but only Allcock, Ashman, Butler and Kennon were regulars in the first team. It was a difficult time and it produced some erratic performances. City won at Cardiff and Grimsby, lost against Huddersfield and Newcastle and dropped a point against Preston and Bury. When Charlton came to Carrow Road in October, however, Swindin must have been quietly satisfied with his side's progress, for they stood fifth in a Division Two table then led by Huddersfield.

Charlton's season had started less well and they were struggling in the bottom quarter with a line-up which also suggested a side in transition. In the event winger Brian Kinsey put Athletic ahead only for an Ord own goal to level matters before half time. In the second half, however, Charlton had it all their own way with two goals from Roy Matthews and another from Edwards. On the terraces that old feeling of instability returned; even worse, the Canaries then had to travel to Stoke to face Dennis Viollet and an ever resurgent Stanley Matthews.

*Norwich City - Kennon; Kelly, Staton; Burton, Ashman, Bell; Oliver, Bryceland, Conway, Allcock, Miller.*

*Charlton Athletic - Wakeham; Sewell, Hewie; Tocknell, Hinton, Ord; Kennedy, Glover, Matthews, Edwards, Kinsey.*

Elsewhere there was a resurgence of sorts, or at least, a minor cascade of new ideas. The Telstar satellite had been launched and Private Eye published, while the Sunday Times produced the first Sunday colour supplement. On television, "That Was The Week That Was" was causing official ructions, controversy and adverse comment, which is another way of saying it was carpingly funny and very, very popular. And there was a major world political crisis centered on Cuba where Krushchev wanted to establish a rocket base against a background of Jack Kennedy's anger and determination to stop him. As a Russian convoy loaded with goodness knows what armaments closed on Cuba and the Americans prepared to blow it out of the water, it seemed we were indeed teetering on the brink of a nuclear holocaust. It was the first time I had sensed a very real feeling

*Terry Allcock*

of tension in the news room, a watching of the clock, a jangling of nerves every time another piece of paper was torn from the telegraph machines and popped into the box. No one knew what might happen. When news finally came through that the Russian convoy had turned away from confrontation, and that the situation had been de-fused, many heads were held momentarily in hands.

I think it was between the Charlton and Stoke matches that Ted Bell took me to one side and asked if I would like to cover Norwich City for the EDP on a regular basis. Naturally, I said yes, though it meant a great deal of time, including nights and weekends, would be taken up in travelling to or from matches, attending them and writing about them. Nevertheless, I was thrilled.

My first match as the EDP's Football Correspondent was the game at Stoke, but as we were not at that point travelling on the team coach it meant a long solo rail journey the day before and an overnight stay at a Stoke hotel. On the Saturday morning, as I was preparing to leave for the ground, there was a phone call from the office in Norwich. According to unconfirmed reports Peterborough United had approached George Swindin to take over the reins at London Road in succession to Jimmy Hagan. Would I have a word with him and phone some quotes to the Pink

Un? I hurried to the Victoria Ground and accosted George as he alighted from the team bus an hour before the match. "I haven't heard from Peterborough," he said. "After all, why should I? It's all newspaper talk." In fact, he told me, he and Mrs Swindin were due to move into their new home in Old Catton in two days' time. I phoned the story to Norwich and it appeared in the Pink U that night: "Swindin Denies Posh Approach."

Somewhat unusually I still have the programme from that game at Stoke with George's comments still scribbled on the back. As for the game, City were turned over rather badly, losing 3-0. And Stanley Matthews? I wrote later in the EDP that he still possessed the power "to create uncertainty and indecision. He flitted in and out of the game as any ageing giant should do, his role, obviously, to create confusion. The Stoke crowd loved him. He was cheered every time he touched the ball, and the unfortunate defender was booed every time he took the ball away from him (and let it be recorded that both Staton and Bell did do this). He wandered casually from right-wing to left-wing, to the centre, and once, even into his own penalty area. And he may as well be credited with the first goal."

*Stoke City - O'Neill; Asprey, Allen; Clamp, Stuart, Skeels; S Matthews, Viollet, Mudie, G Matthews, Ratcliffe.*

*Norwich City - Kennon; Kelly, Staton; Burton, Butler, Bell; Mannion, Allcock, Oliver, Bryceland, Punton.*


A week later Norwich met Sunderland at Carrow Road, which was followed by a long haul to Elland Road to face Leeds. By this time we all knew that George was leaving, anyway, not to join Peterborough but to take over as manager at Cardiff. Either Cardiff had topped the salary he negotiated at Norwich or he saw greater potential at Ninian Park. In any event it was a serious disappointment, for the Canaries, it seemed to me, were just beginning to get their act together again. Instead, there was another interregnum and more interviews with chairman Geoffrey Watling at his office in Tombland. As for George Swindin, he suggested to me a few days later that if the carpets had actually been laid at their new home in Old Catton he might have dismissed Cardiff's offer out of hand. Alas for Norwich, the Swindin carpets were still rolled up. They went straight back on to the removals lorry.

In mid-November, City, and 16,600 spectators, gave George a five-goal farewell by beating Swansea 5-0 in his final game in charge. He shook hands with everyone in the old Press room in the bowels of the gloomy grandstand and looked genuinely regretful at his departure. But this was in the future. First, there was that equally gloomy trip to Leeds.

I had always cast United in a Jeckyll and Hyde role, for although this was not their finest line-up (Lorimer, Madeley, Peacock, Giles and Clarke were still to come) they were already displaying a hard front of determination even if their results had hardly been consistent. Leeds' teams were inevitably prickly and combative and even by 1962 possessed the knack of getting under most peoples' skin. Soon, under Don Revie, they were to become one of the most techically proficient British sides I ever saw, and Paul Madeley one of the most complete defenders; but even then, they were unloveable to all but jubilant Leeds' supporters.

As for the niggly game at Elland Road, Leeds were energetic and determined and chased everything, City intricate and essentially punchless. In the end United won 3-0, but there was little joy anywhere. Leeds were beginning to get their act together and would achieve greater things. Sides in general were beginning to concentrate on denying space to the opposition, on squeezing play and reducing goal chances, and the Italians were experimenting with catanaccio, a sort of 8-2 line-up which made "a forward's life miserable, a centre-half's life easy, and breeds the theory that only the result is important and that defeat is a disgrace." It was all a long away from City's usual free-ranging 4-2-4. Possible plusses on the horizon, however, were that Alf Ramsey was to be appointed manager of the England team while Ron Ashman was to be invited to pick up the reins at Carrow Road. He was an enormously popular choice.

*Leeds United - Sprake; Reaney, Mason, W Bell, Goodwin, Hunter, Hawksby, Bremner, Storrie, Collins, Johanneson.*

*Norwich City - Kennon; Kelly, Worrell, J Bell, Burton, Mullett, Oliver, Bryceland, Allcock, Hill, Miller.*


In the beginning his appointment was simply as "acting" manager, as though the board was not totally sure of the policy of promoting from within the ranks. Ron Ashman was still a member of the playing staff, having made over 600 appearances, and more to the point having been at the club for many years. He knew all the players, and they knew him. Would he have difficulty in imposing discipline on his former mates? Would it all get a bit too pally? Could he learn the managerial job quickly enough? Did something like this run through the board's mind? Possibly, though my feeling at the time was that, deep down, they wanted Ron as manager but they did not want a player-manager. Give him a chance to gain experience as boss, let him get the playing role out of his system, then appoint him as full-time manager. That seemed to be the policy, and in truth it was difficult to disagree with it. In the event, Ron seemed happy enough to take up the gauntlet.

I had a great deal of admiration for Ron Ashman. He was a technically accomplished and very fine left-back, and as a manager a shrewd judge of a player. Some of his signings were inspired, and I remain convinced that if the Canaries ever calculated a managerial transfer Value for Money league table he would be very close to the top. In addition, his relaxed style and droll humour also made him very easy to get on with, and we managed to forge a calm, quiet relationship which remained largely intact even when the going became difficult, which later, of course, it did.

Ron's first season in office opened dramatically. Stoke (with Matthews and McIlroy) were crushed 6-0 at Carrow Road, but a fortnight later the Canaries crashed 7-1 at Sunderland. It produced a "City In Blunderland" headline in the Pink Un. Then winter set in with a vengeance and football throughout the country was frozen out for nearly two months, a period of inactivity which so worried Littlewoods and their punters that a Pools Panel was finally introduced. The Big Chill, it was called, and accurately so. City's 3rd round FA Cup-tie against Blackpool was postponed no less than eleven times. One consequence was that the Pink Un, particularly, was so short of material - local football also being severely restricted - and the means to fill pages, that we had to resort to such devices as using photographs of staff sports reporters engaged in snowball fights outside the office. Came the thaw and things got moving again, City carrying all before them in the Cup by beating Blackpool, Newcastle and Manchester City before drawing Leicester City at Carrow Road in the quarter-final.

The Cup was the sleeping giant of the City fans' ambition. Having once reached the threshold of Wembley, and having had final glory snatched from them, the possibility of a second chance was overwhelmingly exciting. Thus a huge crowd was a certainty; and a huge crowd there certainly was. I fought my way into the South Stand, in order to write something about the experience, and emerged nearly three and a half hours later battered, bruised, and having seen very little of the match. But it mattered not. Leicester won 2-0 and the dream was gone. As for the crowd, it was officially put at 43,984, a ground record. But in truth, I do not know how they knew. At about the same time Ron Ashman was confirmed as manager and he marked the occasion, as it were, by signing a promising local youngster by the name of David Stringer.

*Norwich City - Kennon; Kelly, Thurlow; Burton, Ashman, Mullett; Mannion, Bryceland, Allcock, Hill, Miller.*

*Chelsea - Dunn; Harriss, McCreadie; Venables, Mortimore, Upton; Murray, Tambling, Bridges, Moore, Knox.*

Ashman, like Swindin before him, quickly recognised the need to re-build particularly if, as most fans were urging, City were to launch a determined bid to attain Division One status. In those days it seemed a far off dream, but the manager went about his work with a will and slowly, and despite an apparent lack of cash, new faces began to appear. Among them were wing-halves Ken Hill (Walsall) and Freddie Sharpe (Spurs), forward Gordon Bolland from Millwall, a £30,000 investment, and a young goalkeeper from Wrexham named Kevan Keelan. Most significantly, and thanks to a £20,000 donation from Stan Springall and the Supporters' Club, Ashman also brought to the club an ambitious young goalscorer from Luton by the name of Ron Davies. He cost £35,000, which meant City now possessed a fairly expensive strike force.

David Stringer was a somewhat cheaper acquisition, having arrived at the club from that extraordinary footballing production line, the Alderman Leach School, Gorleston. The school, or rather, its sports staff, seemed to have a knack of turning out good young players, and its achievements were unusual. In addition to David, other lads who signed for League clubs included Brian Boggis (Crystal Palace), Graham Saunders (Coventry), Graham Willis (Norwich City), Mike Bailey and Eddie Stone (Charlton), and Peter Simpson (Arsenal).

One Wednesday in May, 1963, I slipped away from the office and travelled to Wembley for the European Cup Final between Benfica and AC Milan. It was a mid-week afternoon kick-off, and it was said that every Italian restaurant in London and indeed in southern England was closed, for all the waiters were at the match. The look of the stadium certainly suggested that. It was not full, by any means, but there was tremendous enthusiasm. As for the football, British opinion was lukewarm, for it was a long way from the sort of full-blooded encounter we were used to on most Saturdays of the season. Instead, here were two sides closing down space, playing a possession game, biding their time. Compared to the usual huff and puff of the League this was a Sunday afternoon stroll. I have to say I loved it, being fascinated by the patterns they wove on the green stadium grass and by the sheer artistry of players like Rivera and Altafini, Simoes and Eusebio. On a historical note, and unless my memory is playing tricks, I believe both sides also played only three defenders in the back row, a system which at the time of writing (33 years after the event) some managers and writers are now espousing as the cutting edge of modernity.

*Benfica - Pereira; Cavem, Raul, Cruz, Humberto, Coluna, Augusto, Santana, Torres, Eusebio, Simoes.*

*AC Milan - Ghezzi; David, Maldini, Trebbi, Benitez, Trapattoni, Pivatelli, Sani, Altafini, Rivera, Mora.*

My first football scrapbooks, collected shortly after war, were invariably made up of grainy pictures cut from newspapers and invariably showed "through the net" views of my particular heroes, the goalkeepers. Usually they were pictured diving, or occasionally punching. In the days before telescopic lenses the cameramen had to get in close, which meant to the side of, or actually behind, the goalmouth. It had its dangers. I remember EDP cameraman Tony Kemp, sitting near the goalline at Swindon and pointing his camera at the penalty area, being struck on the back of the head by a low, driven corner kick. He did not even see it coming, and despite treatment by George Lee, the City trainer, wore a somewhat bemused expression on his face all the way home and for several days afterwards. Once television cameras began to appear at grounds the photographers had to move, for it was decided they were obstructing the view of advertising hoardings behind the goal. Not that the BBC allowed advertising on their screens, of course. Not officially, anyway. Only occasionally, accidently, and in passing. So the snappers were banned behind goalmouths and they had to retreat to the touchlines and bring their lenses into use.

Ron Davies, a prolific scorer who always brought a buzz to the terraces, highlighted another problem, for many of his scoring headers were initiated so far out from the goal that if the camera was pointing at the goalmouth then Davies himself would not be in the picture. In the end the EDP's experts devised a method to capture goal and goal scorer. They took the picture from the touchline, printed it in a wide, landscape format, and then painted in arrows to indicate Davies at one end and the ball going into the net at the other.

One match in particular caused me particular problems. It was a home game against Newcastle, which City duly won 3-1 even though my Pink Un report, phoned through "live" from the ground while the match was in progress, was decidedly luke warm. Many of the fans were furious. Next week Pink Un cartoonist Harry Banger produced a cartoon of me wearing armour and fielding brickbats, and the entire letters page (headline: "Go Home Bruce Robinson") was devoted to the supporters' revenge. I was savaged, and deservedly so. Nearly 18,000 fans couldn't be wrong; perhaps I'd been at a different game; I ought to take up fiction writing; and so forth. What they did not know was that I had become engaged the day before. Perhaps I had a lot on my mind, and not a lot of

it to do with football. Later, after things quietened down, Ted Bell gave me the cartoon as a souvenir.

PASSING SEASONS     58

*Norwich City - Kennon; Kelly, Mullett; Hill, Butler, Bell; Mannion, Bryceland, Davies, Allcock, Punton.*
*Newcastle United - Hollins; McKinney, Dalton; Markie, Moncur, Iley; Hilley, McGarry, Cummings, Suddick, Taylor.*


Charlton won at Carrow Road with surprising ease (Rose; Hewie, Kinsey; Bailey, Haydock, Tocknell; Kenning, Matthews, Firmani, Edwards, Glover), and then George Swindin re-appeared with a Cardiff team which included ex-City player Dick Scott, the Welsh genius Ivor Allchurch and the great John Charles. Nearly 15,000 fans saw Barry Butler handle Charles exceptionally well, and thanks to three more goals from Ron Davies the Canaries helped themselves to a 5-1 victory. But August, September and October were, by and large, grey, difficult months save for a belated City recovery to a comfortable League position and the shining light of Ron Davies.

Davies was a quiet, dignified, imperturbable lad who because of his scoring ability - he was certainly the best finisher I saw during my Carrow Road days, and if Tommy Lawton was a better header of the ball then he must have been a genius - found himself in the middle of a great deal of national ballyhoo. The Sunday newspapers, who plagued our lives with "floated" stories about players, hardly any of which checked out, constantly suggested he was the subject of big bids by X, Y or even Z. Davies said little, as was his wont, and just kept hitting the back of the net - 30 times in his first season with City, I believe.

Even so, the City fans were restless. Attendances were becoming marginally lower, and there was no longer any interest in attaining a mid-table position. In some ways, it was an anxious time.

*Norwich City - Keelan; Kelly, Thurlow; Hill, Mullett, Sharpe; Mannion, Bryceland, Davies, Bolland, Punton.*
*Middlesbrough - Connachan; Gates, Jones; Townsend, Nurse, Spraggon; Ratcliffe, Gibson, Horsfield, Harris, Braithwaite.*


Two events rocked the world of football world in 1964, one being the start of a programme called "Match of the Day" on BBC TV. The other was the "bribe" scandal, broken by the People newspaper, which initially involved three Sheffield Wednesday players, Peter Swan, Tony Kay and David Layne. Oddly, the go-between, the link between the paper and the story, was ex-Charlton forward Jimmy Gauld. The story sent tremors through the game and probably halted a tiny problem in its tracks. "Match of the Day" was different. No-one knew where it might lead, except that the nightmare scenario of empty grounds and stay-at-home fans was seen to have come a step closer.

The World Cup Finals in England were now only two years' away, and in May I saw the home country beat Uruguay 2-1 at Wembley. It was an uneasy, edgy victory from a team (Banks; Cohen, Wilson; Milne, Monty Norman, Moore; Paine, Greaves, Byrne, Eastham and Charlton) which then bore only a passing resemblance to Sir Alf's final selection in 1966. And a few months later, when England played Wales, World Cup soccer seemed even further away. There was a solid EDP reason for seeing this match, as Wales had selected Ron Davies and his big rival, Wyn Davies, of Bolton, while the England line-up boasted another newcomer with local connections, none other than Mike Bailey, then with Charlton.

Mike, who went to school at Gorleston, was one of a long list of good young players "sold on" by Charlton in their efforts to keep the club afloat. Some clubs, including perhaps Norwich, will always be in the position of being suppliers to the top division, whatever it may be called. I can recall an endless drift from the Valley, in addition to Mike Bailey - Campbell, Bonds, Halom, Bowyer, Robert and Jason Lee, Kenning, Minto, Barness (who they subsequently re-signed); and so on. City fans in recent years have also found that the constant bleeding of young talent can cause accumulative problems. But because of the economics of the game there is little that can be done, except unearth even more talent. Anyway, England v Wales had a Charlton and a Norwich player in the ranks, and there was honour enough in that.

Looking at this England team now, with so little time left before the World Cup, it still seems surprising how far away Ramsey was from his final squad and playing pattern. Here he was playing with Nottingham Forest's Wignall leading the attack, two out and out wingers, and with the creative side largely in the hands of West Ham's Johnny Byrne. But at least Hunt was there, so Sir Alf must at least have been thinking of changing the pattern.

*England - Waiters; Cohen, Thomson; Bailey, Flowers, Young; Thompson, Hunt, Wignall, Byrne, Hinton.*

*Wales - Millington; S Williams, G Williams; Hennessey, England, Hole; Rees, R Davies, W Davies, Allchurch, Jones.*


There is little doubt that Ron Ashman was coming under increasing pressure at the start of the 1964/65 season. The fans' shortening frustration span reflected their own anxieties and City's failure to establish themselves as a real force in Division Two. Attendances were beginning to drift, and that early barometer of customer dissatisfaction - "when are we going to get some new signings?" - was beginning to register on the conciousness and in the columns of our newspapers. What Ron was looking for were young, experienced players at prices he could afford. So was everyone else, of course. Even so, he must have looked forward to the first pre-season friendly match away at St Mirren with a certain amount of pleasure, for it also gave him an opportunity to cast an eye over one or two possibilities. Tommy Bryceland also looked forward to the trip; for him, it was the same as going home.

The fact that City could even consider a pre-season friendly in Scotland was an indication of the development of internal air travel. A lot of it had to do with Air Anglia and its fleet of DC3s, otherwise Dakotas. But that came later. The St Mirren trip was pioneering in a sense that in mid-1964 internal flight services from Norfolk were not particularly well established, so this was a little bit special. It was the first time I had flown with the team squad, and it has stuck in my memory ever since - the trip to Paisley, the hotel at Kilmacolm, and the windswept match, with Vanguards and Viscounts lumbering into nearby Renfrew, sending great shadows sweeping across St Mirren's Love Road pitch every few minutes.

Journalistic travel to City's away games generally depended on the current relationship with the current manager. Most of the travelling was done by rail, or by car if it was a relatively easy distance to drive. If the manager had no objections, then we travelled in the team bus. From our point of view this was by far the best way to do things, because it meant a good standard of hotel - there was new money in the game, and players and clubs were beginning to flex their financial muscles - and proper meals. There was also the point that if I was late arriving at the away ground, at least the team were late, too. I do not recall it happening, though there were one or two close shaves when the coach was held up in heavy traffic or the driver lost his way.

There was another familiar phenomenon. I wrote of autograph hunters: "They hunt in packs, and cover all the entrances and exits of London stations. They know when the teams are travelling through, and what trains they will be on. They have the appropriate pages of their books turned back and dog-earned, ready for presentation. 12.28pm, West Brom due in, to play at White Hart Lane tomorrow. 1.10pm, Norwich City arriving en route for the West. 3.16pm, Chelsea leaving, heading for the Midlands. They meet the trains and chase the tubes from station to station, and patter along beside the players as they manhandle their bags along corridors, up stairs and in restaurant rooms."

And we stared at strange towns through grimy windows. Again, I wrote: "The town is busy and the streets are swarming with traffic. The cinemas blare and the pubs twinkle, and the people look extraordinarily happy. Or confident. We peer at them through the window, these OTHER people. Supporters of THEM. At least, that's how I feel. The players natter happily among themselves, and scarcely seem to notice."

They, of course, lived as a race apart, as the animals in the zoo. But it was still mostly hour upon hour of numbing road travel, chasing after taxis, sleeping in coaches, cups of railway coffee, wandering about in cold hotels or deserted restaurants, hanging about on railway stations. Carlisle away in mid-March is not this East Anglian's idea of pleasure. On one bitter cold occasion I travelled from Norwich to London by rail on Boxing Day, seemingly the only passenger on the train, and struggled through heavy snow and deserted Underground stations to Shepherd's Bush only to find the referee had called off the game 10 minutes' earlier. And Keith Skipper and I once battled through bad weather to get to Watford again to find that the game had also been called off. This time the blizzard was so severe snow was drifting into and piling up in the only phone box we could find outside the ground. But of course, there were compensations.

Soccer was slowly evolving into showbiz, and although at this point the George Best phenomenon, Carnaby Street and trendy flares were still a little way off, the players themselves were beginning to inject a little pizzazz into their lifestyles. We got to know them pretty well, and only occasionally did a grumbling report of an indifferent match cause a surface friction. Usually it was travel, team talks, tea and toast. And killing time. Cards or telly. Light training. Walks. Sitting around in dressing rooms. Playing "golf" at Kilmacolm with pine cones and sticks. Talking about football. Finally the match, and the long haul home. It was on one of these trips I ate scampi for the first time, thinking it scandalously luxurious. As for flying, even crammed into a trembling, vibrating Dakota, it seemed to be the bees' knees.

*St Mirren - Liney; Murray, Wilson; Clark, Clunie, Gray; Quinn, Carroll, Ross, Beck, Robertson.*

*Norwich City - Kennon; Kelly, Mullett; Bradley, Butler, Sutton; Oliver, Bolland, Davies, Bryceland, Punton.*


The arrival on the scene that autumn of wing-half Mal Lucas - almost a Don Pickwick clone in terms of playing style - bolstered one of City's problem areas, placated the fans, and took the club's spending on new players, including Davies and Bolland, to about £150,000, a staggering sum for a Second Divison club at that time. Now the kitty was very low indeed, but at least Lucas proved a marvellous bargain at slightly less than £20,000. He ultimately became a major mid-field influence for several seasons. Stocky, gritty and determined, Mal added long needed bite to the middle area of City's game.

But City's form still fluctuated wildly. Then the side settled into a segment of the table just behind the leaders, clear of the bottom but a little way short of the summit. Attendances fluctuated, too, though perhaps this was only to be expected as several visiting managers raised a menacing ghost by consistently fielding sides with one single-minded ambition - to avoid defeat. Away from home it involved playing for the draw, packing the defence and denying the home side space. It had a debilitating, cloying effect on an entire bloc of Second Division matches. Entertainment was strictly limited, submerged for the common good of the club.

Leyton Orient, for example, came in late autumn and played only two players in attacking positions, pulling their wingers back into mid-field and sometimes even allowing them to operate behind the full-backs. On another infamous occasion I recall a visiting team persuading its players to switch shirts at the last minute, so that they no longer corresponded to the names and numbers in the programme. It was supposed to confuse the opposition and introduce uncertainty into the minds of markers, but in reality it meant that neither the crowd nor the Press knew what was going on. The wrong players were undoubtedly credited with goals and misdemeanors. And so on. Another dodge tried at least once at Carrow Road was the refusal of a visiting side to name any sort of team at all. When they finally took the field only the visiting fans and the visiting Press man knew who they were. The upshot of that little episode was a new regulation which required managers to deliver a team sheet to the referee at least 30 minutes before kick-off.

*Charlton Athletic - Jones; Miller, Kinsey; Bailey, Hewie, Gough; Glover, Matthews, Ryan, Durandt, Peacock.*

*Norwich City - Kennon; Kelly, Mullett; Lucas, Butler, Allcock; Heath, Bolland, Davies, Bryceland, Mannion.*


Crowd trouble was not something that erupted with sudden and unexpected violence. It had always been around the edges of the game, but now it grew again in the conciousness like a virus, seeping into the cracks and crannies. Perhaps it reflected the general restlessness and dissatisfaction of the time. Whatever it was, several incidents from the 1960s and 1970s stick in the mind. I recall Duncan Forbes performing heroics on the platform at Sheffield station, delaying a horde of baying home fans long enough for the City supporters' train to begin to draw out of the station. There was Portman Road, when City fans invaded the pitch at half-time as the Ipswich groundstaff, acting on the referee's orders, attempted to put salt and sand in Hancocks' goalmouth after City, including Keelan, had slipped and slid to a 2-0 deficit on a frosty, quagmire pitch. And I remember Millwall and a raw, bitter day at Cold Blow Lane, when I witnessed vicious hooliganism for the first time. Banter between the two sets of supporters had become progressively more serious. The tone changed from ribaldry to obscenities and then to objects thrown wholly, it has to be said, from the Millwall side. Afterwards, outside the players' entrance, a policeman showed me what the Millwall fans had been throwing. Coins, but not ordinary coins. Someone had filed the rims to a cutting thinness, so that each one was a tiny discus with a razored edge. Several people were injured and someone could easily have been killed. It was incomprehensible. But the Millwall fans had even more up their sleeve. Roving, baying gangs took it into their heads to chase the City fans back on to the Underground, station by station, train by train, right back to Liverpool Street where they finally ran into a barrier of policemen.

The trouble at Cardiff was entirely unexpected. It had been an untidy and increasingly fraught match, not helped by some eccentric refereeing. City were leading 2-0 at half-time and Cardiff hurled everything at the City goal when play resumed. Free-kick followed free-kick and then the home fans, perceiving an anti-Cardiff bias in the official adjudication, started to throw toilet rolls on to the pitch. When the referee threatened to abandon the match if further objects were thrown the announcement was greeted with jeers and laughter.

So the match continued in the same fraught vein. Then the referee left the pitch, apparently having pulled a muscle, leaving a linesman to take over control with the Cardiff trainer running the line. With two minutes to go and City leading 2-1, Cardiff were awarded a penalty by the deputy referee, but Barrie Hole sliced his spot kick and Kevin Keelan palmed it away. Seconds later Gerry Mannion seized possession, rounded Harrington and Williams, and beat Wilson with a crashing drive from outside the penalty area. This time it needed a cavalcade of taxis and a platoon of police motorcycle outriders to see us all safely back to Cardiff station.

*Cardiff City - Wilson; Harrington, Rodrigues; Williams, Murray, Hole; Farrell, King, Tapscott, Ellis, Lewis.*

*Norwich City - Keelan; Kelly, Mullett; Lucas, Butler, Allcock; Heath, Bolland, Davies, Bryceland, Mannion.*

In January, 1965, the Dereham branch of the Norwich City Supporters' Association held its annual dinner at Jentique social club, and I was among those invited, along with Ron Ashman and a coterie of City players. I still have the menu (oxtail soup, salmon, turkey and the trimmings, sherry trifle, etc) which at some point during the evening was autographed by the manager; and although I have forgotten the pleasures of the meal I do recall why they wanted me there. For a week or two I had been suggesting that the Canaries were not ready for promotion to Division One, purely on the basis of their inconsistency and evident lack of cash. Anyway, a bit of an argument had been running through the letters columns of the Pink Un, and the theme was picked up by the speakers at the dinner. It was all fairly friendly, even though Ron might have sucked his teeth a bit when he autographed my card.

Development of the side had reached an interesting stage. Phil Kelly, Mal Lucas and Barry Butler certainly looked good enough for a higher level of game, and Kevin Keelan, after a somewhat shaky beginning during which he struggled with a near post weakness, was beginning to stake out a reputation for himself. In attack, Ron Davies was a good as ever, but Gordon Bolland and Gerry Mannion spluttered like fireworks, and sometimes Terry Allcock, who always played with the upright elegance which was his trademark, had to alternate between defensive and attacking duties. It must be said that Mannion was a match winner when his game was on song, but he often appeared riddled with self doubt.

Behind the scenes at Carrow Road there was a cheerful, clubby atmosphere, much of it generating from chairman Geoffrey Watling. The physio at that time was Billy Furness, who had been with the club many years and who acted as a sort of surrogate father to some of the young players; Bert Westwood ran the office and did his best to balance the often contrary needs of administration, players, Press and supporters; while the pitch, stadium, and the training ground at Trowse, were ruled by the Allison family, particularly Russell, a marvellous character in his own right.

Russell would stomp around the ground grumbling about everything and everyone in sight; but to see him escorting a party of children behind the scenes was to know there was another side to him. I can see Russell now, delving into the antiquated lighting cabinet to sort out some problem, rushing off to some nether region of the ground because he had heard kids were clambering over the wall, cadging a cup of tea in the Press room, grumbling about footballers. I once mentioned I'd see him the following Wednesday, because a Norfolk Senior Cup match was scheduled at Carrow Road. "Bloody amateurs," he said with unexpected vehemence. "Why don't you like amateurs?" I asked in all innocence. "They make bigger slide marks on the grass and cut more divots than the pros," he said. Then the penny dropped. Russell longed for a perfect patch of grass at Carrow Road. Only footballers, paid or not, prevented him from achieving it. Jumping ahead of the story a little, I also recall another little scene played out in the manager's office. I was talking to the boss when Russell stomped in. "What are those players doing on the touchline?" he demanded. "They're going to train on the pitch. It'll be good for them," said the manager. "No they're not," Russell retorted, red in the face. And he told the manager in no uncertain terms what hard work it was getting a good surface and what a drawback it was having footballers who persisted in running about on the grass. "Let's talk about it over a beer," said the manager, fetching two or three bottles out of his cupboard. Half an hour later I left them to it, still talking and sipping their beer. On the pitch, meanwhile, the players were busy running about and doing their training.

As far as the football was concerned Ron Ashman reaffirmed his belief in an attacking game at a time when many other sides were becoming more and more defensive and cautious, and winger Terry Anderson joined the club from Arsenal in a move designed to pep up an attack which was still having scoring problems. But the spectre of inconsistency and financial worry remained for some time. It is also interesting to recall that in those days not only was the Ipswich fixture considered to be a local derby, but those against Leicester City and Northampton Town, presumably because of the boot and shoe manufacturing influence, were known as "derbies" as well. As the footwear industry declined so the "derby" tag faded also, leaving only Ipswich as the old enemy.

*Norwich City - Keelan; Kelly, Mullett; Lucas, Butler, Sutton; Heath, Bryceland, Allcock, Davies, Punton.*

*Northampton - Harvey; Foley, Everitt; Leck, Branston, Kiernan; Walden, Martin, Brown, Leek, Robson.*


Despite the Second Division clubs' "They shall not pass" attitude, and Stanley Matthews' retirement after 33 years in the game, there were some marvellous players around. Don Rogers, Swindon's silky outside-left, was certainly one, and I can still express surprise that he did not carve out an international career for himself. I also recall Bolton's Fred Hill and Wyn Davies, Charlton's Mick Kenning, later to join City, Bristol City's John

Atyeo, Southampton's cutting edge of Chivers, Melia and Sydenham, and Middlesborough's Mel Nurse. There was also something to enjoy in the Jimmy Hill razz-ma-tazz at Coventry, where the club introduced dancing girls, pop requests, loudspeaker interviews and cheerleaders, all aimed at raising the sky blue temperature at Highfield Road. On one occasion City crashed 3-0 against the Sky Blues, but the visit was memorable for something else. It marked David Stringer's League debut.

At the same time there was an instantly forgettable Cup Final, fought to a standstill by those two methodological giants, Liverpool and Leeds. "This was no cultured exhibition of the finer points of the game," I wrote in the EDP, "it was a contest of attrition, of one side wearing down the other until tiredness and exhaustion finally took its toll." Even so, it was one of the noisiest and most atmospheric matches I'd attended: "One end of the stadium burned with the red of a forest fire which even the rain could not douse, and the other was flecked with white. On this occasion it was the snow that melted. Liverpool, in fact, gave what little dignity there was to the game."

*Liverpool - Lawrence; Lawler, Byrne; Strong, Yeats, Stevenson; Callaghan, Hunt, St John, Smith, Thompson.*

*Leeds United - Sprake; Reaney, Bell; Bremner, Charlton, Hunter; Giles, Storrie, Peacock, Collins, Johanneson.*

Football has rarely stood still in tactical terms, even though it has sometimes gone through periods of introspection (in the 1980s, for example, when little that was new was introduced) and fashion (immediately after England's World Cup win, when everyone began to play 4-3-3, come what may, and much of the Second Division football was abyssmal). A simplistic assessment as far as Norwich City are concerned would be to say that Archie Macaulay introduced the "modern" post-war game to the club. Brazil had unveiled their 4-2-4 system in the 1954 World Cup, and Macaulay was one of the first to try it. City's successful Cup formation of 1957/58 was more or less based upon it, using Crowe and Hill in mid-field, two wingers (Crossan and Brennan), with Bly and Allcock in the centre. Five years later Brazil introduced 4-3-3 by the simple expedient of pulling left-winger Zagalo back to take over a mid-field role. By and large, however, British clubs stayed with two in mid-field; certainly George Swindin kept it that way, though it was not always successful because the pair would often be out-numbered. Ron Ashman went through all these "systems," and anguished on what to do next. By September, 1965, even he was tinkering with 4-3-3, playing Stringer, Lucas, Butler and Mullett at the back, with Bryceland, Allcock and Sutton in mid-field. But Ron was never quite sure. After all, he still had the Davies-Bolland partnership to call upon, and he was plainly loath to dismantle it.

Early that winter Alf Ramsey brought his England Under-23s to play France at Carrow Road, a match which saw an emphatic 3-0 England victory and which also drew a crowd of 20,200. Ramsey, however, was clearly unimpressed. His line-up still featured two wingers and retained a basic 4-2-4 shape, yet he was on the verge of switching to three in mid-field and three up front. Interestingly, the only English player on display at Carrow Road that night who was able to make any sort of impact of the World Cup was Alan Ball, later to become the League's first £100,000 transfer when he moved from Blackpool to Everton. One month after this game Ramsey turned out a team in Madrid minus established wingers and with Bobby Charlton in a mid-field role.

*England Under-23 - Stepney; Lawler, Thomson, Hollins, Mobley, Smith, Thompson, Ball, Jones, Chivers, O'Grady.*

*France Under-23 - Heinrich; Merelle, Brucato, Desremeaux, Polny; Andrien, Dogliani; Blanchet, DiNallo, Guinot, Roy.*


Somewhat belatedly the Football Association decided in late 1965 to re-open the debate for and against the abolition of "amateur" status and proposed, instead, the substitution of one category, "player." The heat generated by this argument is difficult to understand now, but up to that point the amateur game had played an influencial and honourable role in the development of football. Witness Pegasus, Bishop Auckland, noble deeds every season in the FA Amateur Cup, Amateur Internationals, and even a British team in various Olympic Games.

The concerns were manifold. If illegal payments were being made, could they be stamped out? If amateur status was abolished, could the amateur clubs survive? There were certainly plenty of rumours - of the player who, on being offered terms by a local part-time professional club, discovered he could make more money as an amateur; the Yarmouth man who told a competition official that in three years he had made over £2000 as an amateur; and of clubs with two balance sheets and a stockpile of "unofficial" cash. Mostly, the traditionalists were merely saddened by the prospect of seeing what had been a wholesome section of the game simply disappear. Oddly enough, once the decision had been made and once the FA Amateur Cup disappeared off the fixture lists, most of the fears and anticipated problems evaporated.

City fans had other concerns, for there began one of those dreaded serials when the Sunday newspapers repeatedly claimed that Ron Davies was on the move (Newcastle seemed to be in frame quite a lot), while the club maintained he was not for sale. Then in January, 1966, Ron Ashman made yet another attempt to resolve his goalscoring problems by signing Hugh Curran, a tough, determined Scot, for £12,000 from Millwall. It was yet another shrewd acquisition by Ashman for yet another relatively modest outlay.

*Preston North End - Kelly; Ross, Smith, Lawton, Singleton, Kendall, Hannigan, Godfrey, Dawson, Spavin, Lee.*

*Norwich City - Keelan; Stringer, Mullett, Hill, Sharpe, Allcock, Anderson, Heath, Davies, Bryceland, Punton.*


Hugh Curran was an instant success. A genuine player, explosive and forthright, he put fire into an attack which hitherto had leaned a little too heavily on the willing and yet fallible shoulders of Davies. In the penalty area Curran was a real handful who "put himself about a bit," as managers were prone to say. But as far as City's season was concerned, his arrival was a little too late. There was a diverting flutter in the FA Cup, with 5th round defeat coming finally and narrowly in a pulsating replay against First Division Blackburn Rovers at Ewood Wood. This was after I spent a couple of days with the team as they prepared for the match, staying at the Norbreck Hydro, Blackpool, where we played five-a-side soccer in the garden. But the League campaign finished on a sullen note, the team finishing in a disappointing 13th position.

There were other problems, too. Cash for new players was in short supply and the fans' morale was low, for the dream of First Division football, nurtured ever since the Canaries had gained promotion, when anything seemed possible, was fading fast. I also became embroiled in an unfortunate argument with City's Supporters' Club and its hard-working secretary, Stan Springall. Shortly before the season ended I suggested in the Pink Un that City, as a side, were not yet good enough to gain promotion, and moreover, that they might not be able to hold their own, financially speaking, in Division One. The City management were a bit sniffy about it but the Supporters' Club, and some Pink Un readers, were downright annoyed. On another tack it seemed to me that the Supporters' Club, ever generous with its hard earned income and in the way it supported the Canaries, was also dissipating its profits by pumping cash into other sports in the area, including cycling, athletics, angling and netball, as well as a number of charitable concerns.

My point was that all the cash ought to go to Carrow Road. Stan's argument was that its fund-raising competitions drew support from all sorts of sports and sports people, and that its founding articles of faith stated the aim that it was to raise money for City and any other sporting association or charity which the committee deemed worthy of support.

*Blackburn Rovers - Else; Wilson, Newton; Sharples, England, Joyce; Darling, Jones, McEvoy, Ferguson, Harrison.*

*Norwich City - Keelan; Stringer, Mullett; Lucas, Sharpe, Allcock; Heath, Bryceland, Bolland, Davies, Punton.*

At the core of the problem was the fact that while players were flexing their financial muscles and salary bills were soaring - even for Second Division clubs like Norwich - attendances at Carrow Road were in serious decline. Six years earlier, in the Third Division South, City's gates hovered around the 30,000 mark. Now the average was down to about 16,000, and once went as low as 10,600. In basic terms, the level of attendance depended solely on City's League position and the attractiveness of the visitors. If City and their visitors were both locked in mid-stream then the fans turned their backs on the turnstiles. This problem also had to be set against the fact that Carrow Road itself was not one of the most modern grounds in the country. A good many cosmetic improvements were made, but there were few seats, the toilets were awful and the refreshment areas drafty and gloomy. It was difficult to see where a catalyst for change was to come from.

By the end of April, when relegation-threatened Charlton came to Carrow Road, I wrote that City's "outward image is changing, and so is the political, tactical and financial structure of the game. And so City, an honest to goodness middle of the road Second Division side, must retain the enthusiasm and vitality of previous seasons or slip gradually, like many others, into the nether regions. They must, between now and next August, recapture the imagination of the public." There was also an increasing meanness spreading through the game and across the terraces which was difficult to define but which was undoubtedly there.Ironically, the future was also out there, on the pitch, right in front of us, in the shape of a robust, workaholic Charlton attacker, a certain R Saunders.

*Norwich City - Keelan; Stringer, Gladwin; Lucas, Mullett, Allcock; Heath, Bryceland, Davies, Curran, Punton.*

*Charlton Athletic - Wright; Bonds, Kinsey; Whitehouse, King, Burridge; Peacock, Saunders, Holton, Kenning, Glover.*

In the spring of 1966, as League form faltered and the fans began to dream instead of World Cup glory, Norwich City were struck two hammer blows. First Barry Butler, the club's stalwart centre-half and lynchpin of the defence for so many season, was killed in a car accident. Barry had been struggling with injuries for some time, but it was assumed he would be ready for the 1966/67 season. Then the board, evidently deciding this was the time to make a change, sacked Ron Ashman. The loss of Butler was a devastating blow, and while some supporters had been clamouring for a change of management I had to confess I was genuinely sorry to see Ron go. Looking back, I am convinced he laid the foundation of City's later history, having largely re-built the Cup side of seven seasons earlier. In terms of his Second Division campaign, inconsistency, lacklustre opponents and a lack of cash undoubtedly hampered him, but on the plus side, the club was an established part of the Divisional furniture. It seemed as though it had required only one more monumental heave to achieve the desired senior status. Instead, Ron left the club after an association of 21 years, and a small part of Carrow Road went with him.

Now the board decided to introduce a New Look and a new approach with a young, ambitious outsider. Enter Lol Morgan, of Darlington fame, then recognised as one of the brightest new lights on the managerial roundabout.

*Bolton Wanderers - Hopkinson; Cooper, Farrimond; Rimmer, Hulme, Beech; Lee, Hatton, W Davies, Greaves, Taylor.*

*Norwich City - Keelan; Stringer, Gladwin; Lucas, Sharpe, Allcock; Heath, Bryceland, R Davies, Curran, Anderson.*


The effect of a long season told on me, too. I was watching 50 games a season - the first team at home and away, reserve games, internationals and Cup finals - which involved hours of travelling and time away from home. There was also the time spent hanging about at Carrow Road, waiting to see someone, dawdling about in the main office trying hard to keep out of Bert Westwood's hair. And hanging about at the Trowse training ground, too, waiting for training to start or finish or the manager to come out of the showers. Seeing so much soccer on such a regular basis also meant the development of a sort of a sixth sense, about a game or a particular player. This is something, I think, that only regular total immersion can do. Oddly, all this exposure also left me with a handicap which persists today, namely, an inability to watch properly, or form any real opinions of a game, unless I am sitting above the centre line. I think it has something to do with the pattern of play. I like to see the tactical pattern, the shape, something I find impossible to do behind a goal where you merely sample the excitement and see the goalmouth action. So a sort of weariness set in at the end of each long campaign, as I am sure it did for the players, too. The World Cup final, however, was too good a chance to miss.

On behalf of the EDP I applied for a Press ticket for Wembley, more in hope than anything else. The reply which came back was non-committal. Would I report to the Press centre on the morning of the match, and take pot luck? Certainly. I travelled to London on the Friday and duly reported to the Press centre early on Saturday morning. Credentials were checked and a precious ticket was handed over, not for the Wembley Press box, which was already filled, but for a Press overflow area in the main stand. After it was all over, and when I got home, drained and emotional, I watched the game again on television with the sound turned down, concluding that it had been a game of fire but no grace, emotion, but little beauty. Even now I remember Moore's calm authority at the back, Tilkowski's eccentric 'keeping, Ball's industry, the abrasion of Stiles, Hurst's opportunism, the interplay of the England front six, and that marvellous moment when Bobby Moore raised his arms and the sun glinted momentarily on the Jules Rimet trophy.

Thirty years later, watching it again on video, it seems to have been a better game than memory allows, fluent and easy paced, free of a cramped mid-field and tackling from the back, with Germany looking marginally the more skilfull side. Still, we had gone to see England win. Everything else was irrelevant.

*England - Banks; Cohen, J Charlton, Moore, Wilson, Stiles, R Charlton, Peters, Ball, Hunt, Hurst.*

*Germany - Tilkowski; Hottges, Schultz, Weber, Schnellinger, Beckenbauer, Haller, Overath, Held, Seeler, Emmerich.*


Lol Morgan arrived at Carrow Road from Darlington three weeks before the World Cup Final, youthful, energetic, aimiable and approachable. Three hours later he had met everyone there was to meet at Carrow Road, held a Press conference, snatched a quick lunch, and accompanied me back to the EDP offices for a brief tour of the building and a glimpse of the back files "to see what you have been saying about the club." I wrote later, "Take heart, City fans, this man has vitality." As far as I was concerned the omens were good and initial preparations for the new season went well. His first "signing" was Alan A'Court, the former England international and Liverpool left-winger, who was to share training and coaching duties with George Lee, a post which Barry Butler might conceivably have filled one day. And when Carrow Road held its first "open house," on a balmy August evening, some 5000 fans turned up and jammed the board room, dressing rooms and corridors, clambered in the Press box, inspected Russell Allison's grass cutting equipment and beseiged the new manager and his players. Everyone was delighted. Then another hammer blow fell.

There had always been a feeling that City might not be able to keep Ron Davies for much longer and that larger clubs were sniffing around. As early as May, for example, Newcastle were said to have offered £50,000. In the end the winning club was Southampton, of the First Division, and the fee, about £60,000. Chairman Geoffrey Watling was in two minds about the whole affair. "I have over a period of time refused offer after offer after offer," he told me, "and even as late at 9pm on Wednesday I turned down a good one; but when Southampton came back with a further offer it was one that we could not refuse." It was a record fee for City, but the loss of Davies was a huge blow to the morale of the fans - many of whom reacted furiously and, of course, blamed Morgan - and a blow to Morgan himself, who I am convinced had little say in the matter. City certainly needed the money to help with team re-building, and Curran's continued good form may have convinced the directors that the loss of Davies might not be too damaging. Already faced with the task of reshaping the defence after the loss of Butler, and having spent the close season working on a 4-3-3 formation, with Bolland, Davies and Curran as the front three, Morgan now found himself beset by problems in all directions. For a number of reasons the season started dismally. To make matters worse, Ipswich won at Carrow Road.

*Norwich City - Keelan; Stringer, Gladwin, Lucas, Sharpe, Allcock, Anderson, Bryceland, Bolland, Curran, Punton.*

*Ipswich Town - Hancock; Mills, Houghton, Harper, Baxter, Lea, Spearritt, Hegan, Crawford, Baker, Brogan.*


Working at away games always embraced an element of risk for Pressmen, not the least being the constant pressure of actually needing to arrive before the kick-off while at the same time placing one's-self in the hands of railway timetables, unexpected traffic jams, or airports closed by fog. I was never actually late for a game, but I did come close to it at Portsmouth, arriving at Fratton Park after an aggravatingly delayed rail journey a mere two minutes before the whistle. For mid-week games the minutes were not quite so critical, for there was always a telephone somewhere, and if the pressure was really on then match reports could be composed on the spot and dictated "live" down the phone to a copy-taker at the office. Saturday games were different, however, for the Pink Un pages were waiting to be filled, and the timetable was very tight.

All soccer scribes have horror stories of their own. Ted Bell once told me of an occasion when Norwich City were playing a non-League side in a Cup game, and he arrived at the ground to be presented with a brick and a long length of cord. Apparently the system was that the reporter wrote his copy, wrapped it round the brick, then lowered it out of the back of the grandstand where it was retrieved by a waiting boy who unwrapped the copy paper and ran to the nearest telephone. I recall two hair-raising incidents, one related to an away match played during a period of industrial trouble involving telephone operators. Some phone exchanges were working, and others were not, and the system had gone haywire. There was no operator to talk to, and for some reason the only direct dial connection I could make was not with the EDP office in Norwich but with an unknown lady in Rickmansworth. Whatever I dialled it was always the lady in Rickmansworth who answered. By the eighth or ninth connection, and against a background of my heightening tension and mumbled apologies, she finally professed a passing interest in the way the match was progressing. Not until early in the second half did I manage to establish a link with a frantic Pink Un staff in Redwell Street who were faced with empty pages, no match report, and time running out.

Another incident which did my blood pressure no good at all was an arrival in a Press box to find that although a booking had been made no phone was available. Nor was there the prospect of one. In the end I had to elicit the assistance of a 15-year-old lad sitting in the grandstand and persuade him, by the simple expedient of offering money, that he would be better employed as my "runner." I believe he made five trips out of the ground, clutching pages of my hasty handwritten scrawl, to a nearby telephone box to phone the copy through to Norwich. There was another moment of panic at a mid-week Combination match at Carrow Road, when there were a few fans on the terraces, only one or two in the grandstand and no-one else at all in the Press box. The goals started to flow with such regularity I dared not blink in case I missed one. When the final whistle went I calculated the result as 6-6, but having no one to check it with or talk to about it finally decided to find the referee. "Was it 6-6?" I asked. "I think so," said the ref, adding, "The players thought so, too, but I was going to have a word with the Press man." I told him I was the Press man. In the end we compared notebooks, and agreed score and scorers.

The Redwell Street office was chaotic and noisy, with lots of clattering up and down concrete steps between editorial and the "stone," where the metal pages were made up. It had an atmosphere and a romance all of its own. The ceaseless clink and chatter of rows of Linotype machines, the smell of moulten lead, printers in aprons working on the shiny "stones," the background tick of teleprinters, cigarette smoke and plastic coffee cups, the constant clack of typewriters and the ringing of phones, and a distant growl and rumble as the press in the bowels of the building began to build speed and spew newspapers into the waiting arms of the sorters.

There were two sorts of football report, the first, the more considered sort when there had been time for thought, and the "running" report, mainly for the Pink Un or for midweek matches, which was made up on the spot and dictated to a copytaker as the match was in progress. The latter was always the easier, for the former meant hours spent agonising over phrases, endlessly re-writing, and Sunday mornings dribbling away toiling over a typewriter. Running reports had another advantage in that the copytaker was invariably Ralph Potter, who had taken Pink Un copy during the Cup campaign of 1958/59 who was so adept he could tell from the crowd noises what sort of game it was. He was also good at anticipating what you were trying to say, and often finished off sentences while I struggled to find the right words. Ralph was a gem, and it was always an enormous relief on a cold afternoon in Carlisle, Middlesbrough or Cardiff, to hear his calm, reassuring tones.

There was no calming effect for Lol, though, as things went from bad to worse. In October, defeat at Rotherham dumped City unceremoniously on the bottom of the Second Division, and even as early as mid-October the letters columns were full of gloomy predictions of relegation. Morgan, meanwhile, was rushing from one match to another in a fractic search for players, and slowly new faces did begin to appear - full-back Alan Black from Sunderland, Laurie "Topper" Brown, from Tottenham, and later centre-forward Laurie Sheffield (Doncaster Rovers) and winger Mike Kenning (Charlton). "Topper" Brown was a great character as well as being a commanding centre-half and, I suppose, Morgan's replacement for Barry Butler. A former Bishop Auckland man and an England and Olympic amateur international, he had turned to the professional game to fill a similar role at Spurs to that of Monty Norman. He was a down to earth, engaging character, with more than a touch of Duncan Forbes about him.

*Rotherham - Hill, Wilcockson, Clish, Rabjohn, Haselden, Tiler, Lyons, Williams, Galley, Casper, Chappell.*

*Norwich City - Keelan; Stringer, Black, Sharpe, Brown, Lucas, Heath, Bryceland, Bolland, Curran, Anderson.*

The period immediately following England's victory in the World Cup was not memorable for the quality of its football. Essentially, the weaknesses of a 4-2-4 formation had been underlined and most clubs were in the process of changing to Ramsey's 4-3-3 or trying something completely different, often with awful results. Some clubs which struggled to play 4-3-3 simply did not have an Alan Ball or a Martin Peters in their line-up and were therefore quite incapable of doing so with any degree of fluency. Others were content to defend in depth, particularly away from home, and concentrate on avoiding defeat. The football was often dire and the level of entertainment very low indeed. And this, coupled with falling gates at Carrow Road and City's inability to make any sort of positive mark on the division led to an increasing twitchiness on all sides of the infernal square - players, fans, board and Press.

At a Supporters' Club presentation night at the Norwood Rooms in Norwich, when Stan Springall handed Geoffrey Watling a cheque for a further £15,000, the chairman revealed they were losing at least £1500 on every home match, adding that the search for new players was still going on. But the club's image had not been helped by the local Press, he said. "When the Press are given advance information with regard to possible transfers, it is wrong of them to give a stream of articles on the progress of the transfers." The Lord Mayor of Norwich, Harry Perry, also waded in: "I long for the days when I can pick up my Pink Un and Eastern Evening News and read constructive criticism of the club written by people who believe in the club's future." Len Votier, of the Supporters' Club, took another tack: the decline in support. "It is not just here in Norwich, but all over. A change in style of play has had something to do with it. Norfolk people want to see good, old fashioned football with five forwards up having a go."

A few days later I hit back in the EDP, defending our journalistic approach and describing the club dinner as an anti-Press jamboree, a kind of literary night of the long knives. A few days later, after some of the dust had settled, Geoffrey telephoned the EDP and suggested a meeting. "At your office, Mr Watling?" we asked. "No, little David will come to you," he replied. I discovered later that when he arrived at Redwell Street he told reception his name was "Mud."

Things were eventually sorted out, of course, because in the end we needed each other. One revelation from the meeting was that City, because of their poor start to the season, now needed 21,500 home gates to break even on the season. Another direct effect of peace breaking out was that the door between the Press room and the Board room was once more unshackled and access to both sides allowed. Geoffrey Watling remained, in my book, a genuine and delightful chairman. And Lol Morgan did eventually begin to turn round the side's fortunes. It passed scarcely without notice, however, that when City fought a glum 0-0 draw at the Valley, Charlton once again fielded their robust and forceful centre-forward, Ron Saunders.

*Charlton Athletic - Wright; Bonds Kinsey, Reeves, King, Appleton, Kenning, Gregory, Saunders, Campbell, Glover.*

*Norwich City - Keelan; Stringer, Mullett, Lucas, Brown, Allcock, Sutton, Bryceland, Bolland, Curran, Anderson.*


Lol Morgan's frantic searching for new players and his endless quest for consistency slowly paid dividends, and the side dragged itself up the table, eventually finishing 11th. But there was no mistaking the continual edge of anxiety that dogged the team's progress and its style of play. Of course there were highlights, but with promotion seemingly out of reach and the memory of bottom place still fresh in supporters' minds, it needed something a little bit special to keep the campaign alive. It came in the shape of the FA Cup.

In January, 1967, Derby County visited Carrow Road in the 3rd round of the Cup, bringing with them a more than useful side including Webster, Saxton, Hector and Durban, and the Rams were fully expected to win. Nevertheless, a 21,300 crowd saw City triumph 3-0, giving one of their best displays under Morgan's guidance. I wrote later: "City's success stemmed from the centre section of the team, from Brown and Allcock at the rear, Lucas and Bolland in the middle, and Sheffield and Curran up front. Around these six the rest of the side circulated and improvised, and for once the real reason for the complex pattern of modern forward play became partially clear, namely, to get a man, with the ball, into open space." On the Monday following the Derby match Lol Morgan, Terry Allcock and Laurie Brown came to the EDP office in Redwell Street to watch the Cup draw for the 4th round come over the teleprinters. The slip of paper eventually chattered over the printers to be torn off and handed to them. Manchester United, at Old Trafford. Gulps, sheepish grins and lots of bravado all round. Later, another slip of paper from the Press Association said that at the Victoria Club call-over, Manchester United had been installed as 11-2 favourites for the Cup. City were listed at "1000-1 and upwards."

The days leading up to the Old Trafford fixture were tense, for injuries to Kenning, Sheffield (groin) and Curran (knee ligaments) threatened to deprive the Canaries of their leading strike force. In the end Kenning declared himself fit, but Sheffield and Curran were not. When the team bus finally set out over the misty Derbyshire Dales bound for an overnight stay at Stockport, the diminutive Don Heath, a Ron Ashman free transfer signing, had been added to the squad. That Friday night I went with Lol and a group of the City players to watch Stockport against Port Vale; then it was early to bed, a late breakfast, and back on the coach again bound for Old Trafford.

There were 63,400 fans there that day, an estimated 10,000 of them from East Anglia - practically every coach and train in the county was called into service - and the result, achieved by a side struggling in mid-table Division Two and deprived of their two leading scorers, must rank as one of the most astonishing one-off performances in the club's history. They were magnificent. What Morgan said to them in the dressing room before the kick-off I do not know, but in the end a screen of yellow shirts protected Keelan while in mid-field the pattern and purpose of United's play was gradually worn down and broken up. In the end, United became more and more desperate, throwing more and more men forward. Rather than try to contain United for the first 30 minutes, City actually went in front. A flick from Bryceland behind Sadler put Heath through, and with United claiming off-side Heath curled the ball past Stepney, rooted on his line. There was continuous frantic activity in the City half, and Law eventually conjured a quite superb equaliser, but as the loudspeakers began to give out details of the replay arrangements it suddenly seemed to dawn on City that United, frantic and fragmented, were actually vulnerable. In the 65th minute a deep lob into the midst of United's now fragile defence seemed harmless enough as Stiles had it covered and Bolland, flailing along behind, seemed to have no chance of success. Then Dunne suddenly cut across Stiles, the ball bobbled into no man's land and Bolland, following through, hammered it into the net. The rest, as they say, was history.

It seems clear now that the loss of two key front players contrived to work in City's favour. With Bryceland and Heath up, City were forced to play a harrying, chasing game, and since the great day I have often wondered what would have happened if Sheffield and Curran had been fit and Morgan had elected to try to carry the game to United.

Anyway, bedlam reigned. Reporters in the dressing room, television inverviews under arc lights, pictures of City players in the bath, and Matt Busby, moist eyed, drawn and disappointed, coming in to shake hands and congratulate everyone. As the City supporters' trains poured out of

Manchester station a huge crowd of disbelieving United fans remained behind to see City board their coach, ringed with policemen. There were a few boos and cheers as we drove off, and then a hearty reception from a large group of Manchester City supporters who happened to be on their way home and who recognised the team. All the way to Derby the coach, driven by the ever cheerful Bill Smith, the team's regular driver, was shadowed by a possee of Press and television cars. At the restaurant in Derby there were more cheers, photographs and congratulations, for by now City were the talk of the country and the nation's Number One sports news item. The restaurant manager was waiting to greet the players. "You want champagne? We have champagne for you." Lol said, "Thank you," delighted with the touching gesture, and corks popped profusely throughout a meal eaten amid a hubbub of excitement and constant requests for interviews.

City's Cup season eventually came to an end when they lost in the 5th round 3-1 to Sheffield Wednesday in front of 41,000 at Carrow Road. And the club duly received a bill for the champagne. I never did discover who paid it.

*Manchester United - Stepney; Dunne, Noble, Crerand, Sadler, Stiles, Ryan, Law, Charlton, Herd, Best.*

*Norwich City - Keelan; Stringer, Mullett, Lucas, Brown, Allcock, Kenning, Heath, Bryceland, Bolland, Anderson.*

Lol Morgan approached the 1967/68 season knowing that pressure was building even before the first ball had been kicked. There was a feeling outside the club that City ought to be in Division One and a feeling inside that this was what they wanted, even though they might not be able to afford it. Completing the circle, however, was immensely difficult and as it turned out, elusive. For one thing gates were hovering in the 14,000 to 19,000 category, depending on opposition, and new players were not available, as they had been in Ashman's day, at prices the club could afford. For another, Morgan's intended team structure of a solid back four fronted by six attackers constantly inter-changing in complex, fluid movements, such as Ramsey had achieved in the 1966 World Cup final, did not really come to pass except on odd occasions. The old warhorse, inconsistency, continued to delay progress.

Slowly, however, Morgan's frantic searching for new faces did pay dividends. Centre-forward John Manning came from Shrewsbury and winger Ken Foggo from West Bromwich Albion. Later, wing-half Gerry Howshall joined City, also from WBA, signing the forms publicly at a supporters' gathering at the Norwood Rooms. He was followed by yet another winger, Charlie Crickmore, from Rotherham. A reserve goalkeeper, Peter Vasper, was also signed from non-League Guildford. City's eight season bill for bringing in players was now about £400,000, an immense sum for a club which had few players to sell (aside from Davies, Monty Norman, Burton and Hill), had difficulty in bringing on its own youngsters, and which leaned heavily on supporters' donations. But by November a City side of some substance was beginning to take shape.

Birmingham were convincingly thrashed at Carrow Road, in City's best performance for a long time, and when Hull were beaten 2-0 at Boothferry Park it seemed that Lol's hard work was paying off at last. Poor Hull. A once mighty club with a ground graced by a fine, new cantilever stand and one of the best pitches around, they were beginning to fret about the possibility of relegation to the Third Division while surrounded by the trappings of success.

*Hull City - Swan; Davidson, Butler, Banks, Wilson, Greenwood, Henderson, Wagstaff, Chilton, Houghton, Wilkinson.*

*Norwich City - Keelan; Stringer, Mullett, Lucas, Brown, Sharpe, Foggo, Bryceland, Manning, Curran, Kenning.*

Most of the time I travelled to away games on the team coach, Morgan being benevolent in outlook and largely unconcerned by the possibility of what others perceived as "potential difficulties." Our relations with players were usually good, though there was an understandable tendancy towards uncommunicative glumness if they had lost or if they thought The Press - local or national - had been unfair or unreasonably hard. Interestingly, the mood was usually collective, and shared by all. Usually, though, we got on reasonably well, most journeys settling into the familiar routine of snoozing, reading newspapers or chatting, more often than not to Morgan, or to George Lee, usually about football. At the hotel on a Saturday morning there was another routine - a light, late breakfast, a meal at midday (steak, scrambled egg or chicken, rice pudding, toast and tea or milk), a rest, then on to the coach again for the last lap to the ground. Most of it was simply tedious, though to them it was as much a part of the game as flogging one's self to exhaustion on the training ground. But 16 hours in a coach all the way to Bristol and back, after finding Ashton Gate waterlogged and the game called off, was enough to try one's patience and physical condition.

The actual reporting of football was more "literary" in those days, with the focus firmly on events on the pitch. For example, I cannot ever remember informing readers about a player's wife having a baby, or how another had decorated his kitchen. Such information was deemed private and of no interest whatever to folk in the EDP circulation area. What did matter was the coming and going of players, the tactics and style of play, the longer term context of a particular result, and an interpretation of current events. Glancing back to the end of the 1960s it seems to me that although players and managers alike were beginning to flex their financial muscles, they had not quite attained full showbiz and personality status. Within five years, however, television and tabloid newspaper wars were to change all that.

So what did a football writer look for at a match? I can only speak for myself. Shape, fluency, movement, style, invention, goals, excitement, entertainment. It is oddly difficult to put into actual words. In a sense it was little more than waiting in the hope of seeing the perfect match. You never did, of course, but in my book players with style, such as Bobby Moore, Martin Peters, Trevor Brooking or Glen Hoddle, or further back, Len Shackleton or Raich Carter, Jimmy Hagan or Eddie Firmani, had the gift of lifting a match out of the mundane and into the intellectual and were well worth waiting for. So perhaps that is what I looked for: something a little bit special, a move or an incident that was anything but commonplace.

This may have seemed strange at a time when methodology, work rate and pace, coupled with a new hard professionalism, fuelled by increasing amounts of cash to winners and economic catastrophe for losers, were beginning to take over. Perhaps this was also the stage when I began to part company with the game. Yet it has always seemed to me that football was a fragile commodity that needed nurturing and protecting, particularly as it was already beginning to change. The first stirrings of an emerging squad game had taken place once substitutions were allowed, initially in the absurd hope that a change would only be made if a player was injured. And as 1967 drew to a close it was also possible to speculate on a future when fans at Carrow Road might have comfortable clubrooms in which to meet and refresh themselves, and stadium seats on which to sit.

*Charlton Athletic - Wright; Curtis, Kinsey, Moore, Went, Reeves, Campbell, Tees, Gregory, Bolland, Peacock.*

*Norwich City - Keelan; Mullett, Black, Lucas, Brown Allcock, Foggo, Bryceland, Manning. Curran, Kenning.*

In January, 1968, City sold Mike Kenning to Wolves for a fee in the region of £40,000, which meant that Morgan had signed Black, Brown, Sheffield,

Kenning, Manning, Foggo, Howshall and Crickmore for about £150,000, and sold Sheffield, Kenning, Heath, Bolland, Davies and Punton for only slightly less. It was disappointing to see Kenning go, but he looked a better player in a better class of football, and slightly ill at ease in the hurly burly of Division Two. It also meant that Lol began yet another year with a question mark against the City attack and major worries with the defence. His "sticking plaster" approach had so far kept the side in the safe regions of mid-table, but there was little sign of actual progress.

Ipswich came to Carrow Road in February (Hancock; Mills, Houghton, Spearritt, Baxter, McNeil, Barnard, Hunt, Crawford, Viljoen, Brogan) and won 4-3, which did little to soothe the City fans' patience, but Southampton were beaten in the FA Cup, and it began to look like yet another season which was to sparkle and fizz like occasional fireworks lit over a long period of time. City were not a bad side, and Lol's search for attacking flexibility had brought some dividends, namely the burly attributes of Hugh Curran, but he was still unable to find the very thing that Ron Ashman had searched for and failed to unearth - consistency.

A team playing badly are difficult to talk to. They tend to turn in upon themselves, close ranks, become uncommunicative and see all non-squad members as a potential threat. But a team not playing badly and still losing are a sad sight to behold. This is a situation the fans do not seem to understand. No doubt the professional approach differs from one sport to another, and I can only speak of my experience of footballers, but I have never known a player take the field intending to play badly, or a team deciding beforehand to lose. Out of tune and out of touch, players can actually try harder than ever and achieve substantially less. Anyway, someone has to lose sometimes; that it the game.

I remember an away match - at Ayresome Park, I think - when City's performance lacked sparkle and they were hammered 4-1. City's travelling band of supporters were particularly indignant that day, and there was booing as the Canaries trailed off the pitch and some abusive chanting outside the ground. Having phoned the last of the sorry news to the Pink Un, I went to the City dressing room. It was a scene of devastation. The players were in various stages of exhaustion, ashen faced and open mouthed, lolling on the benches in frozen attitudes of despair. One player was retching from tiredness, bloodstained bits of cotton wool littered the floor, and the trainers were looking after another who had a nasty bruise on the ribs and was in some pain. I watched as one player wearily took off his mud-caked boots and rolled down his socks. His shinbones were as uneven as zylophones, due to the close attentions of opposing players who over the years had kicked lumps out of him. Blood was trickling over his feet. He looked at me, shrugged his shoulders, and dragged himself off to the bath. All of them wanted to be on their own. Later, when we stumbled aboard the team coach for the long, quiet journey home, a knot of City fans was still waiting and still hurling abuse. One of them spat: "What a shower! They didn't even try." I thought of the blood and the vomit in the dressing room and wished that football was as easy as some of the fans evidently thought.

City's Cup reward for beating Southampton was a 4th round tie against Chelsea at Stamford Bridge. It was not a game in which they were expected to do well, and indeed their first half display, watched by nearly 60,000, did seem to lack commitment. After the break, however, City took the game into the Chelsea half, eventually losing 1-0, a scoreline which looked even narrower as the minutes ticked by.

*Chelsea - Bonetti; Hollins, McCreadie, Boyle, Hinton, Harris, Cooke, Baldwin, Osgood, Birchenall, Tambling.*

*Norwich City - Keelan; Stringer, Black, Lucas, Brown, Sharpe, Foggo, Bryceland, Manning, Curran, Crickmore.*


The season settled into one of modest mid-table success, but with gates hovering around the 16,000 mark this was not the sort of campaign needed to keep interest alive. There was one curious incident towards the tail-end of the season, with City due to play a mid-week match against Crystal Palace at Selhurst Park. The City party, plus myself, were seated in the coach outside Carrow Road waiting for the "off" to London when it was realised John Manning was not there. As the minutes ticked by and the coach driver began to fret about his tight timetable, frantic phone calls were made to Manning's home, Carrow Road was searched, and George Lee and Alan A'Court set off by car to try to find him. All to no avail. Then, as the manager and trainers debated what to do, Tony Woolmer, a reserve player who had only returned to Norwich with the reserves from Oxford at midnight, sauntered into view carrying his boots. Lol leapt from the coach, bundled him on board, and off we went. But City's woes were not over, even then. At Newmarket there was a 45-minute hold-up because of traffic congestion, and at Epping the coach windscreen shattered and we spent the rest of the journey to Selhurst huddled in overcoats. And Palace won 6-0.

A fortnight later, at Cold Blow Lane, City were beaten by a disputed 88th minute goal from Dunphy, leading to such ructions that Millwall thoughtfully provided a police escort to help the team coach make its get-away. Somehow it seemed to sum up the season.

*Millwall - King; Gilchrist, Cripps, Burnett, Kitchener, Plume, Possee, Weller, Jones, Jacks, Dunphy.*
*Norwich City - Vasper; Stringer, Black, Lucas, Brown, Sharpe, Foggo, Anderson, Manning, Curran, McDonald.*

At the start of City's ninth consecutive Division Two season there was a difficult public relations job to be done, for with about £80,000 available to be spent, the public clamouring for new signings and the board becoming increasingly restive, Morgan was beleagured and in some ways isolated. There was even a discordant note in the club's annual balance sheet notes: "The directors are concerned that the manager has not . . . " And so on. Confidence, it seemed, was lacking everywhere. I liked Lol, got on well with him, and agreed which much he did, but it was clear he was beginning to feel the strain. Inevitably, almost reluctantly I suppose, he set off on another hunt for fresh faces to appease the gods. City, and Morgan, needed something special to happen.

Meanwhile, the players reported back for training having trendily sprouted hair during the close season. I noted in the EDP: "Sideburn'd and mustachio'd, they will force Beethoven and Pancho Villa to look to their laurels. Perhaps 'new wave' is not a bad description, after all." With the transfer market virtually at a standstill, the first series of matches also produced some wavy and uncertain results, leaving one to suspect that the club faced another long haul to mid-table respectability. Nevertheless, on the day City beat Sheffield United at Carrow Road, Morgan did confirm reports that he was interested in a centre-half named Duncan Forbes, then with Colchester United.

*Norwich City - Keelan; Payne, Black, Anderson, Stringer, Sharpe, Briggs, O'Donnell, Manning, Curran, Crickmore.*

*Sheffield United - Hodgkinson; Badger, Shaw, Munks, Mallender, Hemsley, Woodward, Fenoughty, Hill, Currie, Reece.*

The fans' irritability finally bubbled to a head at yet another Supporters' Club dinner, when the parent club was handed yet another cheque, this time for £15,000. With 500 guests present, including the manager and the City board, several speakers criticised the general standard of football at Carrow Road, the team, team selection, and recent performances. "Are we going to stay in Division Two or are we going to progress?" one of the speakers asked, adding that "the last home match was one of the worst we have seen since Orient were in the Division." Shortly after this Lol and his wife left the top table and walked out, Lol explaining, "I am walking out in disgust at the abuse directed at me from the top table." It was left to Geoffrey Watling and fellow director Arthur South to appeal for unity and try to patch things up.

It was a painful episode, but in a sense it provided the impetus the fans, rightly or wrongly, wanted to see. There was a flurry of signings, including a raw boned centre-half named Forbes (Colchester), Geoff Butler from Sunderland, who could play in either full-back position, and defender Ken Mallender (Sheffield United). Later, forward Bryan Conlon (Millwall) also signed in. The bad news was that Curran asked for a transfer. One immediate result was a narrow 2-1 defeat at an emotionally charged Villa Park on the very day that Tommy Docherty - who presented himself to assembled Press men afterwards as the epitome of gentleness and modesty - took over the reins to be greeted by the home crowd like a Messiah.

*Aston Villa - Dunn; Wright, Aitken, Edwards, Turnbull, Hole, Ferguson, Broadbent, Godfrey, Martin, B Anderson.*

*Norwich City - Keelan; Stringer, Butler, Howshall, Mallender, T Anderson, Foggo, O'Donnell, Manning, Curran, Forbes.*


Early in 1969 the brittle state of City's football was exposed once again, with comprehensive defeats by West Brom and Millwall and a great deal of football played squarely and cautiously. Against Bolton, Morgan recalled Bryceland for the umpteenth time, switched to three in midfield and three in front, and immediately effected some sort of improvement. But the feeling of optimism was not to last. Hugh Curran, who had been a stalwart and explosive member of the side, but who had asked for a transfer because of a dispute over terms, finally moved to Wolves for £60,000, and a few days' later John Manning joined Crickmore on the transfer list. Then Alan A'Court, who had brought a calm influence to the backroom proceedings, decided to leave to become assistant manager at Crewe.

Morgan was now under immense pressure to bring in even more new faces, and in mid-February he made what turned out to be his final foray into the market, signing the England Under-23 forward Albert Bennett - Albert of the white boots - for £25,000 from Newcastle. It was his 14th signing in two and a half seasons, all made at a total cost of about £280,000 (discounting money received from outward movement). Albert was a good touch player, but like Gerry Howshall his career was dogged by injury, and sadly, I think City saw the best of him for only a short time. Three years later he had to give up the game altogether. In any event City's form still fluctuated, the fans adopted a dog in the manger attitude, and gates hovered in the 12,000 to 14,000 region. It was a glum time.

Little of this could be blamed on Lol. Ever since Ashman's time the club had been unable to produce enough local players of sufficient calibre (despite Stringer, Woolmer, Payne, Howard, Govier, Briggs, et al) to fill gaps which seemed to appear with numbing regularity as the game faced up to the fact that football itself was changing. It was growing up, I suppose, becoming more business-like and less openly enjoyable. Most tactical experiments, which appeared in baffling profusion at this time, involved weakening the front line in order to stiffen the middle or the back, and the football did not always flow. So Lol, whose Carrow Road career represented the gap between the old - in which expression and joy was allowed to play its part, and which was in its death throes at about the time Ron Ashman departed - and the new, had the reins when much of the game was in flux, tactically and professionally, when the old order had been challenged and found wanting and the new had not yet emerged. In hindsight, he had little alternative but to apply the sticking plaster treatment.

*Norwich City - Keelan; Stringer, Butler, Howshall, Mallender, Anderson, Foggo, Bryceland, Conlon, Bennett, Crickmore.*

*Charlton Athletic - Wright; Curtis, Kinsey, Campbell, Keirs, Reeves, Gregory, Treacy, Crawford, Moore, Kenning.*


There were bright spots, of course, even though it was difficult to perceive them. The homely atmosphere of the old place was in the care of some friendly personalities including directors Geoffrey Watling, Henry Robinson and Jimmy Hanly; Bert Westwood and Maurice Lawn kept a meticulous eye on things in the office; Russell Allison ruled the stadium and pitch with a sharp word and a broad grin; Billy Furness was a sort of father figure in the treatment room; and Morgan and George Lee looked after the playing side. As far as the squad was concerned there were some hopeful signs there, too. Keelan was the established first-choice goalkeeper, Stringer and Foggo were regulars and Duncan Forbes and Trevor Howard hovered on the fringes. But in the end it was not enough. Plagued by injuries and inconsistent form, and facing a storm of criticism by all and sundry, City travelled to Fratton Park on April 12 more in frustration than in hope. They duly lost 5-2. Five days later, and after another defeat, this time at Derby, the blow fell. Morgan was sacked.

He had maintained the League status quo, reacted quickly and successfully to an imminent threat of relegation, and upset the odds by winning at Old Trafford. "Since then," I wrote next day, "his task seems to have been one of almost constant repair work, patching a framework which buckled regularly because of the club's inability to produce their own youngsters in sufficient numbers and ability." It was as though his City career stalled early on, possibly through no fault of his own, and he spent the rest of his time trying to catch up. In the end he simply found success expensive and elusive.

Lol himself, though outwardly as cheerful and friendly as ever, was clearly devastated. A few days after the dismissal he and his wife came to visit my family for an evening meal. It turned into a lengthy discussion on "what if" he had done this instead of that, on the vagaries and pitfalls of the game, and on pressure, particularly from the fans. I was left with the distinct impression he needed time - he was still only 37 - to consider what particular path to follow in future. A decade or so later, when I tried to track him down to invite him to a City players' reunion, I learned he had gone out of the game altogether. And he never came to the reunion. City finished the season in 13th position, incidentally, and a few days later Terry Allcock, the old warhorse, who had been a majestic forward, a tireless mid-fielder and an elegant defender, was given a free transfer.

*Portsmouth - Milkins; Travers, Ley, Pointer, Tindall, Hand, McCann, Atkins, Hiron, Bromley, Jennings.*

*Norwich City - Vasper; Stringer, Butler, Howshall, Mallender, Lucas, Foggo, Bennett, Allcock, O'Donnell, Howard.*


It was back to caretaker management and interviews in Geoffrey Watling's office in Tombland. We gleaned little from them, I must say, other than the board's determination to get the right man for the job. As the summer drifted on a great many names were bandied about - Jimmy Scoular (Cardiff), Charlie Hurley (Bolton) and Bob Stokoe (Carlisle). Other names included Alan Ball (senior, that is, then at Halifax), Dave Ewing, the former Manchester City player, and of course Terry Allcock, who applied for the vacancy and who was, I believe, interviewed. In the end, and in a somewhat audacious move, the man they went for was Bill McGarry, then manager of Wolves, a bid which surprised and intrigued the football world on two counts, first, that terms had actually been agreed, which meant they had offered him as much or perhaps more than the First Division club, and second, that they were evidently prepared to take on a senior club.

In the end McGarry turned them down, but Mr Watling was far from being downhearted. "The world hasn't fallen apart," he told me. "We are still after other people." And so they were, even though they were running out of time. George Lee took over pre-season training duties - he had taken charge for City's last game of the previous season, switched to a 3-3-4 formation and beaten Blackburn 3-1 in front of a miserly 9250 spectators - and the fans held their breath. Then a mere fortnight before the first game of the season at Villa Park the new man was unveiled - Ron Saunders, latterly manager of Oxford and a former Charlton centre-forward.

Meanwhile, there was time for a brief excursion to Wembley to watch England demolish Scotland 4-1 and a fond, lasting recollection of fine English attacking play, Bremner's spirit, Henderson's surging runs and Bobby Charlton's supremely artistic performance. Then it was back to the coal face.

*England - Banks; Newton, Cooper, Mullery, Labone, Moore, Lee, Ball, Charlton, Hurst, Peters.*

*Scotland - Herriot; McCreadie, Gemmell, Murdock, McNeill, Grieg, Henderson, Bremner, Stein, Gilzean, Gray.*


Ron Saunders arrived at Carrow Road at about the time men first landed on the moon, but he was a man with his feet firmly on the ground. By the time I met him, a few hours after he arrived in the city, he had already made an initial assessment. I felt strongly he knew exactly what he was going to do and the way he was going to do it. He perceived he had little money to spend and thus little chance of challenging the big boys at their own game. Therefore, he reasoned, in order to reach Division One, City would have to be fitter and better organised than everyone else. They would have to be mean, hate to lose or give away a goal, and they would play 4-3-3.

He also realised early on, I think, that a number of established players would not fit the new format, for he wanted organisation before flair and work-rate more than delicacy. So he drove them hard in training, at Trowse and up and down the slopes of St James' Hill on Mousehold - the "pain barrier" was a phrase which came into common use at about this time - then rushed back to the ground and laboured in the neat, windowless office which was once the Press tea room.

Saunders was "brisk and business-like; a mite awe-inspiring and yet immensely likeable," I wrote later. "No nonsense, no frills. Unmistakably the boss. . . He speaks in staccato phrases which roll from the tongue, carefully sifted and pre-packaged, leaving little verbiage for the journalist to prune. And it is he, rather than the journalist, who runs the interview, answering questions almost as a boss dictates to a secretary. 'You can splash this,' he will say, indicating with his hands a size of headline roughly the width of two EDP broadsheet pages, leaving no doubt he expects the printers to comply. 'And you can say that . . . '" And so on.

We were quick to sort out a working relationship. He told me nearly everything that was going on at the club on condition I used nothing until he was ready. And he made it plain that if I wrote something he did not like, "I'll tell you about it in no uncertain terms, but I'll buy you a beer afterwards." In fact, and for all his plans, Saunders bided his time. Fulham and Rotherham were beaten in pre-season friendly matches and City, with Keelan at his gymnastic best, unexpectedly won the first match 1-0 at Villa Park against Tiler, Ferguson, Bruce Rioch - and Tommy Docherty, of course. There was a new, determined attitude about City's play, but by mid-September niggling problems were being discussed in the newspaper columns - City's inability to score goals in reasonable numbers, the poor quality and staggering dullness of the Second Division as a whole, an increase in disruptive on-field practices, and a further downward trend in Carrow Road gates. Nevertheless, Ron decided to make his first move in the transfer market, signing Peter Silvester, a rangy, thoughtful forward from Third Division Reading, for £25,000.

*Birmingham City - Herriot; Martin, Thomson, Beard, Robinson, Pendrey, Murray, Hockey, Hateley, Vincent, Summerill.*

*Norwich City - Keelan; Stringer, Butler, Mallender, Forbes, Anderson, Foggo, Bryceland, Silvester, Bennett, Crickmore.*


And still he bided his time. Scoring problems continued to hamper progress, though on the other hand City were not conceding many, either. But rumblings of discontent could still be heard. In late November I made the point that the football had become too serious, so lacking in fun, commenting: "The last game I went to with a light heart and left humming was an Amateur Cup-tie at Britannia Barracks last season. But of course, the players' jobs did not hang on the result." Ron was unapologetic. "Give us time," he would say. "Nothing worth while is ever achieved overnight."

That same month he made another move, though in a sense it was forced on him by injuries to Foggo and Bryceland and by Crickmore's slip from favour. At Millwall (then a more than useful side with Kitchener, Possee, Gordon Bolland, Weller, Dunphy and the legendary Harry Cripps) he switched to 4-3-3, just as he had said he intended to do, with Lucas, Briggs and Paddon in mid-field and Silvester, Conlon and Bennett in front. City lost 1-0, giving a somewhat static performance in the raw, earthy surroundings of Cold Blow Lane, but the move was significant in that rarely again did he depart from it to any great degree. Now he had two tasks - fine tuning the tactics, and sorting out the personnel.

Bolton were beaten narrowly, Charlton (Wright; Booth, Kinsey, Campbell, Burkett, Reeves, Gregory, Treacy, Riddick, Moore, Masiello) thrashed them at the Valley, they thrashed Leicester 3-0, and then they were drawn at home against Fourth Division Wrexham in the 3rd round of the FA Cup. A few days before the game Saunders found himself without Keelan, who had broken his arm, Silvester, who had influenza, and with plenty of spare tickets on his hands. In the end only 13,500 fans turned up, the Wrexham contingent, so it was jokingly said later, travelling in a mini-bus. But at least they

*Ron Saunders*

witnessed a major upset. Wrexham, playing a game based on elementary geometry and a lot of aggression, and inspired by their tireless 6ft 3in attacking centre-half, Eddie May, so upset City's applecart that the Welsh side deservedly won 2-1.

For Saunders, and as it turned out, for the club, too, it was an important time. Indeed, it could be argued that the games at Millwall and against Wrexham represented a defining moment in the Canaries' history, for in the ignomy of defeat Saunders now knew he had to make changes in personnel if he was to keep to his own timetable. He was, after all, half way there. Forbes and Stringer were forging a formidable partnership at the back, Keelan was firmly established, Foggo and Black were settling in and displaying a rare consistency, the often under-rated but ultimately influencial local lad Max Briggs was becoming a regular, and another new face, Graham Paddon (Coventry), remarkable for his long, flowing blonde hair, was beginning to develop his tireless mid-field game. Wrexham apart, City were generally difficult to beat and conceding few goals. Few sides managed to dominate them. But the make-up of the front six was still not right and Saunders was worried the moment might pass if he did not do something.

On January 27, 1970, he shocked the club's supporters by placing seven players on the transfer list - Ken Mallender, Terry Anderson, Albert Bennett, Charlie Crickmore, Tommy Bryceland, Painter and McDonald. Inevitably, the move was dubbed a Mammoth Winter Clearance, or the January Sales.

*Norwich City - Vasper; Butler, Black, Stringer, Forbes, Lucas, Briggs, Foggo, Conlon, Howard, Paddon.*

*Wrexham - Gaskell; Mason, Bermingham, Davis, May, Evans, Moir, Park, Smith, Kinsey, Griffiths.*


The sidelining of Tommy Bryceland was a huge blow to the City fans who had warmed to his ball-playing skills and tenacity for many seasons. The fact that he had also been pushed out by the club seemed incomprehensible. Tommy, however, was not a 90-minute player. In some ways he belonged to the old creative school, flitting here and there, pausing, flicking a shrewd ball out to his winger, in the manner of the traditional inside-forward. And whereas I shall forever remember the way he heroically harried and niggled Nobby Stiles for 90 minutes during the memorable Cup win at Old Trafford, it has to be said that Alan Ball he was not. But this was what Ron wanted, workaholic dynamos. Nevertheless, Tommy's departure from the club was as melancholy as the breakup of the Beatles, and for me marked the end of the game's immediate post-war era.

Meanwhile, Ron plodded on and City's honest toil began to show results. Mal Lucas and Bryan Conlon were added to the transfer list in March, swelling the number of potential departures to nine, while the manager experimented with a busy Briggs-Howard-Paddon midfield. By April I was able to write that they were playing "with rhythm and a combative resilience" which surprised a number of sides during the tail end of that particular campaign. Keelan, in majestic form, was now among the top three 'keepers in the Division, and Forbes and Stringer were improving with every game. But scoring was still a problem - until Birmingham came for the last home game of the season, that is. City scored six and finished in 11th position, jubilant fans flooded across the pitch to greet their heroes, and Duncan Forbes received the Player of the Year Trophy.

*Norwich City - Keelan; Butler, Black, Stringer, Forbes, Howard, Briggs, Bennett, Silvester, Paddon, Foggo.*

*Birmingham City - Latchford; Murray, Martin, Pendrey, Robinson, Beard, Hockey, Vincent, Vowden, Page, Summerill.*

The Cup Final that year was a bit special. Chelsea eventually beat Leeds 2-1 in a replay after the two sides had drawn 2-2 at Wembley in what I thought was a magical match. Five years earlier Leeds had lost one of the most boring Finals ever against Liverpool, but in the intervening time they had surmounted the criticism, refined their playing system, and flowered as a ruthless yet entertaining side. Some of the muscularity still lurked, but on good days there was also a lavish ration of skill. This particular match suggested to me that if Leeds were a bulldozer driven by responsive hands, then Chelsea were a rapier, eager to attack, willing to take risks. Which they did.

In some ways 1970 was a curious time for the game. England failed in their bid to retain the World Cup in Mexico, prompting Alf Ramsey's comment that there was nothing to be learned from Brazil's style of play or, presumably, from their 4-1 victory over Italy (Pele 2, Jairzinho 2) in the final. Seeing television pictures of the event, I recall gasping at Pele's silky skills, being astonished at the ability of Brazil's players to "bend" the ball in flight, and disappointed by England's inability to change their style of play when it seemed obvious they needed to do so.

This was one of the problems of 4-3-3 as it was played then. Its weakness was that it had deadened the national game and alienated many of the fans; its strength was that it controlled the centre. Played badly, however, it simply choked the middle of the park with players and stifled entertainment and it could, and sometimes did in Division Two, produce the unedifying spectacle of 20 players in a tight ruck chasing one unfortunate ball. In essence, City were now locked on to the 4-3-3 course: a tight and unyielding back four, a tirelessly hard working midfield, the engine of the side, and a front three prepared to work as hard when they were not in possession and when they were.

There was a small postscript to the Cup Final. A week or so earlier the EDP and its sister newspapers had moved from Redwell Street to its new headquarters at Prospect House, and on April 29, 1970, Her Royal Highness the Princess Alexandra came to perform the official opening ceremony. During her tour of the building afterwards she came into the sports department and I was introduced as the EDP's football writer.

"Did you go to the Cup Final?" she asked.

"Yes, ma'm."

"Are you going to the replay?"

One side of me wanted to say that my request to do just that had been turned down by the Editor on grounds of time and expense. But I replied, lamely, "Too busy to get away, ma'm." She smiled wanly, and passed on.

*Chelsea - Bonetti; Webb, McCreadie, Hollins, Dempsey, Harris, Baldwin, Houseman, Osgood, Hutchinson, Cooke.*

*Leeds - Sprake; Madeley, Cooper, Bremner, Charlton, Hunter, Lorimer, Clarke, Jones, Giles, Gray.*

The 1970/71 season started inauspiciously in that Billy Furness retired as physiotherapist - being replaced by Jeff Granger - while an exotic pre-season tour to South America was called off an hour before the party was due to leave Carrow Road for Heathrow. Instead, they went to Yugoslavia. And there were concerns over attendances, which had virtually halved since 1959/60, from about 26,200 to 13,700. But Ron was unyielding in his determination to do things his way. There were tough training sessions at Trowse and on Mousehold Heath and a clear commitment to 4-3-3 with emphasis on hard work and combination. City drew against Portsmouth, and at Luton, and struggled against Chester in the  League Cup, allowing the sceptics to suck their lips and nod their heads and say, "I told you so." Scoring remained the problem, but at least, slowly and perhaps unsurely, City were beginning to suggest they were increasingly difficult to beat.

Saunders was now actively searching for an additional forward and at least one deal, with Bolton's John Byrom, fell down only at the last minute after the clubs had agreed terms of about £25,000. It was a long night, I recall. Byrom and his family reached Carrow Road at about 10.45pm for talks which went on until midnight. In the morning, however, Byrom said, "No." Saunders muttered under his breath, "It's not the end of the world." But it did mean he had to start again.

*Norwich City - Keelan; Butler, Black, Stringer, Forbes, Howard, Briggs, Bennett, Silvester, Paddon, Foggo.*

*Charlton Athletic - Wright; Curtis, Booth, Moore, Went, Reeves, Davies, Hunt, Riddick, Campbell, Peacock.*

City's ability to squeeze and stifle opponents was becoming more apparent, but they were still not dominating the Division, they were not scoring many goals, and it highlighted a problem which I for one never really resolved. Which is the most important, entertainment or the result? I wanted to be entertained. Ron wanted results, even to the extent that he was quite prepared to accept 1-0 or 0-0 scorelines even if they were alienating the fans. In point of fact the Carrow Road faithful were still, to an extent, keeping their distance, waiting to be convinced. It made for some difficult times in the manager's office. Another boring 0-0 draw, I would say. Another point, he would say. I found it a difficult thing to deal with.

In late November the manager made a sudden transfer swoop which, if memory serves me, led to another late night wait in Bert Westwood's office while the deal was being hammered out next door. This time the player said "yes," and midfielder Doug Livermore joined the Canaries from Liverpool for about £20,000. It was another building block put into place. By the turn of the year City were at least in the top half of the table, a mere six points behind the leaders, and there were thoughts that perhaps they could do something if they got on a run. But it was all conjecture.

*Bristol City - Gibson; Jacobs, Drysdale, Wimshurst, Rooks, Parr, Skirton, Garland, Galley, Gow, Sharpe.*

*Norwich City - Keelan; Payne, Black, Stringer, Forbes, Briggs, Livermore, Silvester, Howard, Paddon, Foggo.*

In 1971 I caught up with Laurie Brown once again, this time in his capacity of manager of King's Lynn, thus following in the footsteps of Ray Garrett and Len Richley and making yet another stop on a long footballing journey which had taken him to the Walks via Bishop Auckland, the 1960 Rome Olympics, Northampton, Tottenham, Arsenal, Norwich, Bradford Park Avenue and Altrincham. Laurie's brief was to do the groundwork to prepare the Linnets, from a financial and a footballing point of view, for an application to join the Football League. He calculated then that Lynn needed regular 4500 gates to make them viable in the Fourth Division. Alas, all this also became mere conjecture, just as it did at neighbouring Fenland Park, where the affairs of Wisbech were being managed by another ex-international, Jesse Pye, whom I interviewed several times.

It was a long journey for both of them which in League terms was ultimately unfruitful, but at least they tried. We at Eastern Counties Newspapers (as the company was now called) were undertaking some long journeys, too. Ron Saunders was unlike Ron Ashman and Lol Morgan in that he felt a wider separation of Press and player was better for all concerned, and mostly he preferred us not to travel on the team coach. Indeed, after some occasionally acrimonious disagreements he banned us from travelling on the team coach. This meant we - and by now my compatriot from the Eastern Evening News was a certain Keith Skipper - had to get to away matches as best we could, by car and rail, and later on by air, using Air Anglia's DC-3 services to Bristol, Leeds, and so on. Keith and I spent hours together killing time on lumbering train journeys, talking football, chatting to some of City's travelling army of fans, and playing a version of shove-ha'penny football on ideally-sized train tables, using a penny, two two-bob pieces and a couple of combs. Keith was fond of a long ball strategy while I played more of a passing game, but honours finished about even. Even so, travelling back from Middlesborough, or changing trains in the early hours of Sunday morning, was not my idea of fun.

There were memorable times in the air, too, and flights to and from Carlisle, Birmingham, Portsmouth, Middlesbrough, Manchester, Newcastle, Glasgow and Liverpool. In addition, I recall the plane taking-off from Bristol, climbing over the Bristol Channel and in the process passing from twilight to night and then back from night to twilight as the pilot circled and set course for Norwich. Perhaps the most hair-raising journey was from Leeds. City had been playing at Elland Road in a mid-week Cup replay, and throughout the second half thick banks of fog began to gather. Afterwards, we all piled on the team coach (this was one occasion I was travelling with them) only to be told that Leeds airfield was closed and there was no possibility of take-off. With no other option the coach headed for the centre of Leeds - it was now about 11.30pm - to try to find a hotel able to take 25 people at short notice. None of them could do anything. Finally, in desperation, the coach edged its way gingerly through the fog back to the airport with some fond notion that perhaps we could kip down in the airport lounge prior to a take-off early next morning. Suddenly a message came that there was a clearance "window" and that the DC-3 was waiting on the peri-track with engines running. The coach, escorted by an airport vehicle ringed with flashing lights, nudged its way through the gloom along airport roads until we finally found the plane. Next problem was that there were no steps. This time George Lee came to the rescue, organising some of the team to pile the kit hampers against the side of the door. And thus it was that we managed to clamber up the side of the hampers and get on board. Finally, the hampers were hauled up and secured, we all held our breath, and the Dakota took off. Ten minutes into the flight the pilot sent a message back to say Leeds airport was closed again; had we been 10 minutes later we would have slept in the lounge. On another occasion, returning from Cardiff, we landed at Norwich Airport to see lines of ambulances, fire engines and police cars waiting. After we disembarked they announced that someone had phoned Cardiff Airport to say there was a bomb on board. Thankfully, it was a hoax.

One aspect of professional football which travelling with the team did enable me to witness  as the nervous tension engendered by an approaching kick-off. It is something the fans do not often take into account, but in my experience it is a factor and it affects different players in different

*The author (left) with Evening News writer Keith Skipper queue for the Canaries' special DC3 flight from Norwich to Carlisle in 1971.*

ways. There would be a feeling of slight tension at the hotel, particularly when they were preparing to leave for the ground, and more pangs of nervousness when the team coach arrived at the ground, leaving some of them tight-lipped and quiet, others noisy and animated. Most players told me that once a game started they never thought about nerves, and that the tension drained away. But it was certainly there beforehand.

*Middlesbrough - Whigham; Smith, Jones, Moody, Gates, Maddren, Downing, McMordie, McIlmoyle, Hickton, Laidlaw.*

*Norwich City - Keelan; Payne, Black, Stringer, Forbes, Anderson, Livermore, Silvester, Howard, Paddon, Foggo.*

City's faltering season revived sufficiently in the final phase to push them towards the fringes of the promotion race, but they were always outsiders, unconsidered but increasingly difficult to beat. The City fans were less sanguine and gates wobbled between 9,500 and 13,000, not enough to keep the treasurer free from frowns. It was something that always annoyed Ron Saunders, who could see results improving but no improvement in the level of support. It seemed to me that many of the fans, brought up on the polished intricacies of City's Cup side of the 1950s and the skills of Jimmy Hill, Tommy Bryceland, Bobby Brennan and Ron Davies, simply did not take to the relentless grind of many of the matches being played in the Second Division and the credo that, never mind the entertainment, another 0-0 draw is a point gained and a defeat avoided. They wanted success, but they also wanted football with a smiling face; Ron suggested they could not have both. If the fans were desperate for success then they would have to support the blood and toil. Space was being closed down generally around the Division, and time was always at a premium. No one had a moment to dwell on the ball or slow things down. It was mostly helter skelter, usually in the middle of the park, allied to tactics designed to stop the opposition playing.

   In point of fact, and not to make too much of a thing of it, Ron was already very close to getting the formula he wanted. Keelan was resplendant in goal - one of the finest takers of the high cross, and one of the most acrobatic reflex goalkeepers I ever saw - while Clive Payne and the rest of the back row, Forbes, Stringer and Black, were thoroughly established. Doug Livermore, Paddon and Ken Foggo, meanwhile, represented the backbone of the front six. So progress was being made. In April, 1971, I was able to point out in the Pink Un that while City had won few games at a canter, only twice, at Molineaux and Ayresome Park, had they been thrashed. In other words, they were clearly becoming difficult to beat, something which, again, did not necessarily thrill the supporters. In fact, only 11,436 watched the defeat of Sunderland at Carrow Road.

   Even so, the end of the season which saw Leeds beaten in the Cup at Colchester and involved in a disgraceful melee with WBA at Elland Road, when Ray Tinkler was unlucky enough to be the referee, and Arsenal win the double, also saw City finish in 10th place, one position better than the previous term.

   *Norwich City - Keelan; Payne, Black, Stringer, Forbes, Anderson, Darling, Silvester, Livermore, Paddon, Foggo.*

   *Sunderland - Montgomery; Malone, Irwin, Harvey, Pitt, McGiven, Tueart, Park, Watson, Harris, Hughes.*


   Saunders clearly needed another one or two attacking players to add impetus to his third, crucial season. But he had little or no money to play with, and the fans were unconvinced, or showing signs of boredom, for season ticket sales were flagging. The only alternative was to reduce the wage bill, and this he did during the close season. Ken Mallender and Gerry Howshall, neither of whom had figured greatly in his plans, were among those who left. The effect of all this was that City began the season with the previous year's line-up and the hope that one or two home grown players, such as Paul Cheesley, might make the grade. In fact they began well, grinding out a number of good results and keeping defeats to a minimum. Again, it was not pretty, but it was pretty effective.

In September the dissatisfaction of some of the fans finally bubbled over when anonymous leaflets calling for a mass boycott of Carrow Road's fixture against Oxford made an appearance in the city. Headed, "Campaign for a Striker," the leaflets gave no indication of source, but in strident language they demanded the signing "of at least one striker. The time for excuses and talking is over - we must act now!" Geoffrey Watling was furious and Ron Saunders quietly vexed, but it was hard to decide if the boycott call was serious or if it was a hoax. In any event the short-lived campaign failed. The gate at the Oxford game was 13,749, which was a slight increase, while City won 3-2 and actually went to the top of the Division Two table. Now Ron was getting the results he wanted and gates which were actually beginning to rise as the fans came to terms with the Canaries' sudden elevated position.

Sensing, perhaps, that this was the moment the board loosened the purse strings, and on October 6, 1971, Saunders paid out a club record fee of £40,000 for David Cross, a striker from Rochdale. The papers were actually signed during the City v Carlisle League Cup match, which City won 4-1, the loudspeakers warning the crowd before the end that an important announcement was imminent. When they were told Cross had signed bands of joyful supporters spilled over the pitch and chanted outside the main entrance. Saunders' patience had paid off. About 17,700 had watched the Carlisle game, while 23,000 saw the next 0-0 draw against QPR.

*Norwich City - Keelan; Payne, Butler, Stringer, Forbes, Anderson, Howard, Silvester, Livermore, Paddon, Foggo.*

*Oxford United - Kearns; Lucas, Shuker, Roberts, C Clarke, Thompson, D Clarke, G Atkinson, Skeen, Cassidy, R Atkinson.*


It was hard to believe, but by November City were six points clear of the third placed club and still leading the Second Division pack. Moreover, they were beginning to play like genuine contenders. Burnley were trounced 3-0 and Luton 3-1, and the end to City's long unbeaten run did not come until the 16th match, at Cold Blow Lane, a hard, punishing game which Millwall won 2-1. But enthusiasm was building. The supporters' fund-raising pool added a thousand new members in a month, the attendance average climbed to about 23,000, and even British Rail caught the excitement of the moment by deciding to run "specials" to some of the away matches. When City beat Grimsby at Carrow Road they attracted the highest gate of the season thus far, 27,531.

City's success had another effect, too, for we had an increase in visits to the old wooden Press box by gangs of Fleet Street's finest, who invariably commented on its quaintness and antiquity. This contrasted nicely with the box at Birmingham where an elderly gentlemen always greeted arrivals, showed them to their seat and sorted out the telephones. I had always assumed he was a Press steward. He turned out to be a reporter from the Smethwick Telephone.

Doyen of the Carrow Road Press box for many years was Ted Chamberlin, who prefixed everything with, "dear boy." Three or four minutes after someone had scored Ted would turn and ask, "I say, dear boy, who got that one?" It was a question on which we sometimes took a concensus decision, particularly if uncertainty reigned. Three would say was Cross, five that perhaps Foggo got a touch. So Foggo it was. But Ted was a calming influence on everyone. After a particularly torrid encounter he would ask one and all, "I say, dear boy, wasn't that all a bit lacklustre?" On Saturdays, when he was doing a live radio report, he would arrive with a large clipboard and spend several minutes scribbling before the actual kick-off. If you looked over his shoulder you could see that all he had written was, "Good afternoon from Carrow Road . . . " Once City hit the upper reaches of the Division then we had the likes of David Miller, Donald Saunders, Brian Scovell and Brian Glanville cheerfully putting up with the uncomfortable reality of our little glass fronted world. Clement Freud used to pay occasional visits too, invariably asking who-ever was using the open phone line to the Pink Un office to check the latest racing results.

One day a large, familiar figure appeared, clumping up the wooden steps to the back of the grandstand and seating himself quietly in the corner of the box. It was Sam Bartram, then writing for the Sunday People. The fans seated outside the box seemed to take no notice or even indicate they knew who he was, and from my seat on the back row I used to look at his broad back and shoulders and think that this was a man who had played over 600 League and Cup games (and 200 more during the war), who was never dropped from the Charlton team in 22 years, who made two war-time appearances for England, who played in two Cup Finals (or four in a row, again, if you count the war-time competitions), managed two League clubs, and who in his prime would not have thought twice about performing before 70,000 fans packed into the Valley or Highbury or Wembley. Now the fans did not seem to know him, and I thought how hard it must be for a former player to cope with things like that. Down in the old Press room I'd shake his hand - though I never once told him he was my boyhood hero - and fetch him a cup of tea. He seemed still, quiet, utterly unassuming, even defeated. He simply watched the game, spoke to very few people, sat in the Press room afterwards and sipped his tea, then walked to Thorpe station to catch the train back to London. I suppose I recall this happening half a dozen times. Then he seemed to disappear from the scene almost as suddenly as he had appeared, and I never saw him again. I believe Sam died in 1981.

*Norwich City - Keelan; Payne, Butler, Stringer, Govier, Anderson, Livermore, Silvester, Howard, Paddon, Foggo.*

*Grimsby - Wainman; Worthington, Gray, Smith, Wigginton, Rathbone, Brace, Lewis, Tees, Hickman, Boylen.*


The life of a football manager is never easy, and City's attempts to stay ahead of the pack suffered a serious blow when Duncan Forbes damaged a hamstring. Duncan had become an integral part of the side, as powerful a character in the dressing room as he was on the pitch. A player who might be described as strong and hard, a big bodily presence in the attacking danger areas just inside and outside the box, and a firm header of the ball, his influence, if it could ever be evaluated, might have been worth as much as a goal a game. He projected such an outgoing personality that the atmosphere of a room, a dressing room, or a team coach changed immediately he entered, and this, coupled with his sense of fun and cheeriness, meant that the side, on and off the pitch, seemed flat without him. I think he did for City what Nobby Stiles did for England in 1966. He lifted their spirits. Duncan was a good laugh and a genuine character, always ready with a gentle gibe. I never once heard him grumble about match reports or anything anyone had written. He had a knack of making such matters seem unimportant. Instead, I have several recollections of strolling through the centre of some town or other (Carlisle, Middlesborough, Preston, it matters not), killing time on a Saturday morning before the midday meal and the coach to the match, and being verbally accosted from the other side of the street, and above the noise of the traffic, by a voice at full volume booming, "Helloooooo, Bruce . . . . !" causing shoppers to stop and turn to see what was going on. In fact, his partnership at the back with the modest David Stringer was the platform from which City launched their promotion bid. It's importance cannot be exaggerated. Chalk and cheese off the field, they played as a unit on it.

So Duncan's absence for several weeks at such a critical time of this most important season was a devastating blow. Saunders' first reaction was to bring Steve Govier into the frame, and then Terry Anderson who, as a former out-and-out winger, displayed remarkable powers of adaptation first as a wing-half and then a defender. Later, Ron hedged his bets by borrowing an additional centre-half, Bobby Bell, from Crystal Palace. He also sprang a neat surprise by signing utility player Phil Hubbard from Lincoln City for £20,000 on Christmas Eve. It was a surprise in as much that the EDP and EEN sports staff were enjoying a pre-Yuletide lunchtime drink in a pub in Ber Street when the phone call came through from the Evening News sports desk. It took us 20 minutes or so to convince Keith Skipper that the phone call might not after all be a hoax and that he really ought to return to the office to investigate. In the end he did, and got a story for his trouble.

Such was the growing enthusiasm of the fans prior to Christmas, 1971, that City clicked up their best League gate (31,041) for 10 years, and impressively, 300 of them turned up at Trowse on Christmas morning merely to watch the squad train. A week or two earlier there had been another exciting attraction with a visit by First Division Chelsea in the quarter-finals of the League Cup. Some 35,900 spectators packed Carrow Road but City, minus Cross, Forbes and Govier, also lost Stringer for a time following a nasty collision with Osgood, and ended with Anderson and Howard in back row roles. They lost 1-0, but it was a close run thing.

*Norwich City - Keelan; Payne, Butler, Stringer, Anderson, Briggs, Livermore, Silvester, Howard, Paddon, Foggo.*

*Chelsea - Bonetti; Boyle, Harris, Hollins, Dempsey, Webb, Cooke, Baldwin, Osgood, Hudson, Houseman.*


At the turn of the year an elementary calculation suggested that City needed a point a game to achieve First Division status, though a number of sides, including Millwall, QPR and Sunderland, were chasing hard. Saunders was under no illusions. Promotion was far from a foregone conclusion. Nor were City universally loved. Fleet Street at large seemed to feel City's lofty position was a momentary abberation, and many of the fans took the somewhat grudging attitude that, well, City owe us this one. I recall one saying, "We've supported them through thick and thin, and there's been lots of thin."

By mid-January the squad was indeed beginning to look somewhat jaded, and Hull came to Carrow Road and won 3-0, raising all the old nightmares of possible failure and yet another season to be remembered only for what might have been. Saunders, however, remained adamant that promotion was the goal. He even managed a gentle sideswipe at his murmering critics by suggesting some of the fans were not pulling their weight. Then in February, 1972, Peter Silvester suffered a cartilage injury. A few days later City's closest challengers, Millwall, drew 2-2 at Carrow Road in front of a 34,100 crowd. The loss of a point might have dented City's case rather more than it actually did had not Blackpool unexpectedly beaten QPR. The door was still open.

*Norwich City - Keelan; Payne, Black, Stringer, Anderson, Hubbard, Livermore, Silvester, Cross, Paddon, Foggo.*

*Charlton Athletic - Dunn; Bruck, Warman, Bond, Went, Shipperley, Davies, Treacy, Hunt, Rogers, Peacock.*


Though it was not always pretty to watch, City were nevertheless displaying a steely determination which despite periodic setbacks seemed to hold them in good stead for the run-in. There was a problem in the front line, however, and for a time Saunders even had to abandon 4-3-3 and withdraw an extra man into midfield, thus disturbing the formation which had served the club so well. It was well known, however, that he was chasing all over the UK looking for replacements at a price he could afford, and in March a shoal of red herrings finally turned into the fish he wanted - Jimmy Bone, signed for £30,000 from Partick Thistle, a player who, thanks to his zestful determination, unleashed just the sort of explosive forward runs the side had been lacking. It turned out to be an inspired piece of business.

When City crashed 4-0 against Birmingham at St Andrew's all the uncertainties were raised yet again. Sunderland came and took a point, and only a late burst enabled City to take the points against Hull. Now it was City, and not Millwall or Birmingham, who were being set the questions and asked the justify their position. And towards the end of March they did. Blackpool came to Carrow Road, lost 5-1, and were run ragged by a City side which at long last actually looked like prospective champions. And on April 2 they went to the Valley and won 2-0. Now everything was back on course again, and only a last-gasp disaster could prevent them from going up.

And Charlton? City's victory somehow seemed to emphasise the difference between the two clubs. I wrote: "From half-time onwards an air of inevitability about the result hung like a heavy cloud over the vast and largely empty Valley. Thick-thighed and leaden slow at the back, Charlton had no adequate answer to City's punching attacks." The gate that day was about 12,500, the Valley a crumbling reminder of what it had once been. Huge tracts of the terraces were deserted and the side was playing with a sort of stumbling lethargy usually associated with lost causes.

Inevitably there were City fluctuations to come, including the loss of a point at Shepherd's Bush, but when Swindon came to Carrow Road and were beaten 1-0, and when 31,736 fans shouted and celebrated and sang, "You'll never walk alone," the Canaries were left needing two points from two matches to make promotion a certainty.

*Queen's Park Rangers - Parkes; Clement, Gillard, Busby, Evans, Hazell, O'Rourke, Francis, Leach, Ferguson, Salvage.*

*Norwich City - Keelan; Payne, Black, Stringer, Forbes, Briggs, Livermore, Bone, Cross, Paddon, Foggo.*


April 24, 1972. And so in the end it all boiled down to Leyton Orient and Brisbane Road, London, E.10. Thousands made the journey, Keith Skipper and I travelling in a photographer colleague's car. It was a scene I shall never forget. Yellow and green adorned vehicles swarmed towards London - reminding me that Saunders had once contemplated trying to change City's first choice colours into an all-red strip - while at Brisbane Road the Orient's red and white favours were brushed aside by a tide of East Anglian enthusiasm.

In the end, and thanks to goals from Foggo and Paddon, a penalty, City won 2-1 and at last banished all the doubts and worries, pessimism and scorn. Loved or unloved, glamorous or not, City were in Division One and Ron Saunders stood at the front of the Brisbane Road stand to accept the plaudits of the crowd. City fans swarmed over the barriers and across the pitch; the players clung to each other in mutually shared joy; champagne appeared in the directors' box; "On the ball, City," welled around the ground; the fans sang "For he's a jolly good fellow," and a tide of emotion such as the Canaries had not seen since 1958/59 surged and lapped around the ground. Later, the City dressing room was beseiged by Press pundits and television presenters and cameras, and trainer George Lee was picked up by the players and flung bodily into the bath. Outside in the streets of E.10 the celebrating went on, and it was hours before the straggling column of fans began to think about making its way home. Once all the interviewing and telephoning was done Keith and I slipped away from Brisbane Road, drove a short way home and then stopped for a pint. The pub was full of City fans. Every pub, it seemed, was full of City fans. Anyway, we were recognised and soon drawn into the party, in the middle of which another shining faced City fan arrived only to dump a big clod of earth on the bar. He was triumphant. "It's the penalty spot," he said. I have often wondered what happened to that famous lump of grass.

*Leyton Orient - Goddard; Arber, Hoadley, Bennett, Harris, Allen, Lazarus, Brisley, Bullock, Walley, Bowyer.*

*Norwich City - Keelan; Payne, Black, Stringer, Forbes, Briggs, Livermore, Bone, Cross, Paddon, Foggo.*


There was one other ceremony to perform - clinching the championship; one point needed and one game in which to do it, at Watford. In the end between 8000 and 10,000 City fans made the journey by car, coach and rail, and the irony of the situation could not have been plainer. City were heading for the twinkling lights and heady excesses of Division One, Watford, already relegated, towards the shadows of Division Three. So the stage was set for a curious encounter, half funeral, half party. In the end the Canaries drew 1-1 and the championship belonged to Norwich City and Ron Saunders. Afterwards, it was the familiar story of champagne in the dressing room, interviews, a media hubbub and joyous fans. Later, I found Watford manager George Kirby in a quieter corner of the main stand. "We should have won," he claimed, but without conviction or acrimony. And Norwich? "They're a good side. If you've got teamwork you've got everything, and they've got teamwork." Mike Kenning, by then a Watford player, was there, too. "The ball hasn't been running for us, but that's the way it goes. You have to have luck in this game." Then the Watford players combed their hair and sidled home to tea while the City players and their wives boarded coaches to head for a celebration dinner at Newmarket.

Reflecting on matters a few days later I wrote that City "began unloved and they ended still largely unrated, except by their own fans and by managers who acknowledged their strength of character and resolute approach." Because of early deficiencies in the squad, and a lack of money, Saunders had "decided that City's game would have to be founded on selfless effort and on method. He gave them a grinding and effective consistency." As for the fans, "it was not always enough, for 10 years of tedium had eroded enthusiasm and interest to a point where it was fashionable to be pessimistic. But the yardstick of 1959 is outmoded and no longer viable (individualism having long given way to organisation); entertainment, or a lack of it, certainly came into the reckoning but even this, once Christmas was past, became irrelevant when weighed against the prospect of promotion."

It was that old dilemma raising its head again, except that this time Ron Saunders had proved he was right.
*Watford - Rankin; Welbourne, Williams, Lees, Franks, Eddy, Wigg, Kenning, Jennings, Lindsay, Farley.*
*Norwich City - Keelan; Payne, Black, Stringer, Forbes, Briggs, Livermore, Bone, Cross, Paddon, Foggo.*


Even the Cup Final, at the tail end of this remarkable season, was a memorable if not stylish effort, Leeds' effectiveness overcoming Arsenal's lack of invention 1-0 in front of 100,000 at Wembley. It was all part of the hype, the power game, the television translation of the hero into the personality, and by and large it was enthralling to watch. In an odd way it was also an introduction to what City were facing the following season, and a sort of farewell to Division Two.

It was strangely difficult to say goodbye, despite the lassitude and glumness which cloyed the 1960s Division like sticky toffee, because it was also goodbye to Scunthorpe and Bury, with its delightful, blue ground, Plymouth, Northampton and Bolton, as sad and homely as they come, and the places and pubs we once visited.

Of course, Division Two had its moments. Laurie Sheffield's remarkable debut hat-trick, Gerry Mannion's extraordinary goal at Cardiff, the gloom on the team coach after they had been thrashed 6-0 by Crystal Palace. There was Tommy Docherty's salute to the hysterical terraces at Villa Park in 1969, and the day all the Press phones went dead. Rotherham, with the loudest loudspeakers I had ever heard, and Walsall, where the manager and half the board happily gave up a morning to show me round the ground. Luton's manager walking slowly back to the dressing room knowing the Hatters were relegated, the sadness surrounding the departures of Lol Morgan and Ron Ashman, the day-to-day rumours and intrigues, yesterday's men in the form of former players standing forlorn and half forgotten at Trowse watching today's crop of youngsters train, and the anguish of youngsters being told they were not going to make it.

I remembered, too: "Press rooms, boxes and benches, hard, narrow, bone pinching things, most of them; numbed fingers fighting with a frozen phone dial, the other hand holding a notebook and pencil flapping in the wind; voice and ear struggling to make sense of things against a wall of noise. Hours of staring at the passing night through coach/car/train windows; empty Sunday stations, returning from the North with nothing to eat; the players' card games; the smell of embrocation and steam from the baths, the chaos, the cursing, the blood-stained cottonwool, the recriminations, the socks and shirts, muddied and wet, tossed anywhere and everywhere; and shinbones as bumpy as Elm Hill cobbles, the trademark of the professional player." Loved it. Loathed it. Would not have missed it for the worlds.

*Arsenal - Barnett; Rice, McNab, Storey, McLintock, Simpson, Armstrong, Ball, George, Radford, Graham.*

*Leeds United - Harvey; Reaney, Madeley, Bremner, Charlton, Hunter, Lorimer, Clarke, Jones, Giles, Gray.*

Division One was a party, a celebration of the club's new found status, a reward for all the lean years. The players felt they had earned it and the long-suffering fans felt they deserved it, and there was little time or inclination to think much beyond that. There were, however, a few pre-season harum-scarums. First, the prices at Carrow Road went up. Season tickets, which had cost between £7 and £11 the previous season, now cost from £12 to £18, a substantial rise at a time of rapidly rising prices everywhere. Then there were reports that Coventry wanted Ron Saunders as manager to replace the sacked Noel Cantwell. Elsewhere, the club tried hard to smarten its image. Sharp suits for the first team playing squad, a new determination to provide television reporters with whatever time and facilities they needed, an enlarged Press box, a few new turnstiles to cope with the extra crowds, and even some additional toilets.

There were also worries in some circles about the financial viability of it all. If all the season tickets were sold, if gates were maintained at a 30,000-plus level, and if not too many players were signed, then the Canaries might squeeze through. It was a delicate calculation: be cautious and risk relegation, throw caution to the winds, sign players and risk financial oblivion.

Discussing the quandary, I wrote before the season started: "What it often amounts to is the spending of the season ticket money as soon as it comes in, and sometimes, the spending of next season's season ticket money, too. But a move like this would traditionally go against the City grain, and certainly against the sober financial line followed so successfully since the financial crisis of the 1950s." Set against the club's more recent history, the statement has a curious resonance.

Suddenly it was back to pre-season training at Trowse and on Mousehold Heath, in front of the television cameras, friendly matches, and the prospect of the real thing. On August 10, and as though to allay some of the the fans' fears (there had been no close season signings, remember) , Saunders accepted a new four-year contract. At the same time chairman Geoffrey

Watling announced the police had accepted a 40,000 crowd limit at Carrow Road. The stage seemed set for the celebration.

Everton were the distinguished visitors for the first ever First Division fixture at Carrow Road, and City earned a creditable 1-1 draw. So far so good, we thought. But the gate was only 28,028, causing those of a financial bent to glance at each other and wonder what the future really held. "Mystery of the missing 10,000," was the headline on my soccer notes the following week. Bert Westwood was happy with all the arrangements, saying the bulk of the crowd had been admitted in about an hour, but 28,000 was hardly a proper test of the ground's procedures. Ron had a more forthright comment about the gate: "Disgusting." The level of support was to puzzle and disappoint him for the rest of his stay at Carrow Road.

*Norwich City - Keelan; Payne, Butler, Stringer, Forbes, Briggs, Livermore, Bone, Cross, Paddon, Anderson.*

*Everton - Lawson; Newton, McLoughlan, Kendall, Kenyon, Lyons, Husband, Bernard, Royle, Harvey, Connolly.*


We also wondered how City's promotion winning squad would adapt to the extra pace and class, and the answer is it did its best. But the threadbare state of the club's resources was glimpsed when another newspaper described Saunders' reliance on the old guard as "brave." Ron read it and grimmaced. "I'm not brave," he explained, "I'm just short of money." When he did make a move, however, it was back to old friends St Mirren for the largely unknown forward Jim Blair. Alas for Blair, he cracked a bone in his foot a few weeks after arriving. Nevertheless, there was a feeling City might scape through for a second term. There was an extraordinary 3-2 victory over Arsenal (a crowd of 32,273 for that one; **Arsenal** - Barnett; Rice, McNab, Storey, McLintock, Roberts, Marinello, Ball, Radford, Kennedy, Graham), and a useful draw against powerful Derby County. There were also reminders of the scale of the mountain City faced. **Leeds'** fitful brilliance (Harvey; Reaney, Cherry, Bremner, Charlton, Hunter, Lorimer, Clarke, Jordan, Giles, Gray) earned United a 2-0 victory at Elland Road and City a few compliments for their sterling struggle; but at Upton Park they were played off the park, West Ham's jewels glittering sufficiently in the mud to deserve a 4-0 victory.

This match was memorable for the performance not of City, hard as they battled, but for the play in the Hammers' mid-field of Bobby Moore, who ran the game like a traffic policeman at a busy junction. Unruffled and in his own time, he repeatedly read City's forward movements so quickly that he had intercepted and launched a counter-attack before City realised they had lost possession. As I wrote later, Moore "was as constantly noticeable as a Red Guard at a Hunt Ball. He was West Ham's mainspring, their inspiration, and whatever his detractors may say he towered over this match as I have not seen a single player do for many years." I thought he was quite brilliant, and along with Paul Madeley, one of the best defenders I had ever seen.

*West Ham - Grotier; McDowell, Lampard, Bonds, Taylor, Moore, Tyler, Best, Holland, Brooking, Robson.*

*Norwich City - Keelan; Payne, Butler, Anderson, Forbes, Briggs, Livermore, Bone, Cross, Paddon, O'Donnell.*


Despite the influence of the Division in which they now found themselves, the prestige and the pressure, City still managed to retain something of the atmosphere of the old club. Carrow Road was still Carrow Road, all wood and girders, concrete, gloom and dubious toilets. Physiotherapist Billy Furness had gone, but some familiar faces were still around. Maurice Lawn was still helping Bert Westwood in the office, Terry Allcock was on the coaching staff, along with George Lee, and Russell Allison still cared for his beloved pitch as the Allison family had done for decades. Even so, some things were changing. There were more stewards around, more curbs on the Press, more restrictions, and a new breed of breezy businessman beginning to appear on the fringes of the club. We could not wander into the boardroom any more, as we had done for years. At the same time there was also a new confidence, a spring in the step that had not been there for a long, long time; since the late 1950s and early 1960s, in fact. This was another facet of the success of Saunders' reign.

For several weeks, too, there were promising displays on the pitch, a 2-1 defeat of Tottenham at Carrow Road being a prime example. Spurs (Jennings; Kinnear, Knowles, Naylor, England, Beal, Gilzean, Perryman, Chivers, Peters, Coates) came "like kings to tread among the cabbages," and in front of an ecstatic 34,555 crowd they were deservedly beaten. Cross, who hailed from Rochdale, looked the best forward on the field, I recall. Two weeks later Liverpool came to Carrow Road, attracting an attendance of 36,625, which must have delighted even the sceptical Ron Saunders. In the first half City seemed to stand off and admire their opponents, but it was a different story after the break. They went after them as equals. In the end the game finished at 1-1, extending City's unbeaten home League run to 29 games. Afterwards, in the Press room, Ron tackled Fleet Street's finest about their apparent reluctance to give City the praise he felt they deserved. "Liverpool are a good side, Ron," suggested one experienced hack. So are we, Ron replied. "Well, I thought they looked a great side in the first half." But we looked a great side in the second half. "Yes, you can really play." Then why don't you say so more often in your papers?

All City wanted was to be loved. As for Liverpool, I thought them "the best we have seen so far; more subtle than Arsenal, more persistent that West Ham, collectively better than Derby, more efficient than Tottenham, and in some ways more graceful, too." As the region began to think about buying Christmas cards and presents, so City at least looked capable of earning a second season in the First Division. Even so, one London correspondent said of them: "Norwich's football is as functional as a tin-opener. Every situation, it seems, has a required formation . . . any hint of relaxation brings an earful of Scots oaths from Sgt. Major Forbes."

*Norwich City - Keelan; Payne, Butler, Stringer, Forbes, Briggs, Livermore, Bone, Cross, Paddon, Anderson.*

*Liverpool - Clemence; Lawler, Lindsay, Smith, Lloyd, Thompson, Keegan, Cormack, Heighway, Boersma, Callaghan.*


Imperceptively, however, holes were beginning to appear. In November Clive Payne, who had been keeping Alan Black out of the side, broke two bones in his ankle. Jim Blair was simularly incapacitated and Peter Silvester had to go into hospital for a knee operation. Then on a night of high drama at Highbury, when Graham Paddon scored a marvellous hat-trick and Arsenal (Barnett; Rice, McNab, Storey, McLintock, Simpson, Marinello, Ball, Radford, George, Kelly) were beaten 3-0 in the quarter-finals of the League Cup, Forbes had to leave the field with damaged ribs and a collapsed lung. Despite the heady euphoria and sudden talk of Wembley and Europe, City's resources were beginning to look decidedly threadbare.

Inevitably, performances began to suffer even if the League Cup semi-final draw a few days later (Chelsea v Norwich; Wolves or Blackpool v Liverpool or Tottenham) did momentarily raise the spirit. There was little or no respite. Manchester United won 2-0 at Carrow Road (gate: 35,913) and Chelsea, limbering up for the Cup-tie, won 3-1 at Stamford Bridge. On Boxing Day, when Arsenal gained revenge by winning 2-0 at Highbury in the League, it was clear the last few months of the season were, after all, to be concerned with a battle against relegation.

*Norwich City - Keelan; Butler, Black, Stringer, Govier, Briggs, Livermore, Cheesley, Cross, Paddon, Anderson.*

*Manchester United - Stepney; O'Neill, Dunne, Morgan, Sadler, Buchan, Young, MacDougall, Charlton, Davies, Moore.*

Of course, there were distractions. On a dark night in December City went to Stamford Bridge for the first leg of their League Cup semi-final with the pundits and the formbook suggesting defeat and little option but to try to take the game by the scruff of the neck. Which is precisely what they did. Chelsea, unimaginative and strangely lacklustre, were rocked by two goals from City in the space of 60 seconds. First Bone blasted the ball by Phillips from 20 yards as Chelsea dithered and then Cross, from the edge of the box, scored with a blistering shot in off the underside of the bar. Chelsea were frantic, of course, and Keelan, Stringer and company performed heroics to keep them at bay. So City took a two goal advantage to Carrow Road for the second leg, and thus stood closer to Wembley than they had ever been before. It was a memorable night. Fleet Street's finest were stunned to silence, and City players who usually attracted little attention - Max Briggs, Steve Govier, Alan Black, Terry Anderson - found themselves the focus of widespread interest.

But the real drama was yet to come. On Wednesday, December 22, Chelsea came to Carrow Road for the second leg. There was some concern about the game because fog had been gathering behind the floodlights ever since they were switched on. Slowly, as the second half unfolded, with City leading 3-2 (and 5-2 on aggregate), banks of mist rolled across the pitch and forced a stoppage. The end came in the 84th minute, with City six minutes from an appearance in the final at Wembley. Everyone was stunned, and when the referee and players went off - by this time even the centre circle was barely discernible - no one knew what was happening. There was chaos in the Press box. A huge crowd was pressed around the box standing and wondering and metaphorically gnashing its teeth in anguish, and it was impossible to get out, never mind reach the dressing rooms or the referee. My office wanted to know what was happening, and wanted the story; we wanted the official announcement, we wanted quotes, and Fleet Street was furious at being stuck in City's homely box. In the end I managed to establish a link with "downstairs" through an outside phone line and Carrow Road's main office. It was 20 minutes before we managed to fight a way through the throng to talk to the distraught City players and a distressed Ron Saunders who, in the parlance of the day, announced himself throughly "gutted."

Officially the match had been abandoned, and in fairness to the referee it must be said he did absolutely the right thing. By mid-way through the second half, football was not theoretically possible that night. But City were left in limbo, still clutching their 2-0 first leg lead, and it was not until January 3, 1973, that the replay could be arranged and Dave Stringer could resume his by now legendary sequence of duels with Peter Osgood. In essence, City had to do it all over again, and this they did, Steve Govier's 50th minute header from Paddon's corner sealing Chelsea's fate and sending City to Wembley with a 3-0 aggregate. The fans spilled over the pitch, the City players were mobbed, and "there was nothing left but the singing, the celebrating, and a tumult of a memorable night." I felt enormously proud of them.

*Norwich City - Keelan; Butler, Black, Stringer, Govier, Briggs, Livermore, Cheesley, Cross, Paddon, Anderson.*

*Chelsea - Bonetti; Locke, Harriss, Hollins, Dempsey, Webb, Baldwin, Hudson, Osgood, Kember, Garland.*

In January, Kenny Foggo, one of the heroes of the promotion season but unable to establish himself in the First Division side, signed for Portsmouth. But City were still struggling to hold their own in the League, despite switching to 4-4-2 simply to gain the extra man in mid-field. By now they had been sucked into the relegation zone, and even the prospect of a trip to Wembley could not gloss over the fact that their senior status was at risk. In February, Saunders moved quickly to plug some of the gaps. First, he signed forward Colin Suggett from West Bromwich Albion for a Canaries' record fee of £75,000, and then he persuaded Sheffield United's fiery Welsh international mid-fielder Trevor Hockey to make the move to Carrow Road. Hockey was with the club for only three months, but his influence was profound. He took over a holding role in front of the back four, bringing an ascerbic determination to everything he did, stiffening resistence in a key area of City's game. Later Jim Bone, his scoring impetus largely gone, was to make the reverse journey to Bramall Lane.

Despite the preparations for Wembley, City were dangerously low in the table and totally exposed, as Leeds found at Elland Road, thrashing City 5-0 in the FA Cup. And when they began the road journey to Wembley, safe in the knowledge they were set for the day of their lives, City occupied 21st position in Division One. It was a curious time.

*Leeds United - Harvey; Reaney, Cherry, Bremner, Madeley, Hunter, Lorimer, Clarke, Jones, Giles, Bates.*

*Norwich City - Keelan; Payne, Butler, Stringer, Forbes, Howard, Livermore, Bone, Cross, Paddon, Anderson.*

The great day of Wembley finally came, Saunders naming his team several days in advance of the match. With Suggett and Hockey ineligible and Bone and Foggo gone, the big surprise was his inclusion of Jim Blair, who had suffered a number of injuries and made only one full appearance for City since his arrival from St Mirren. There were alternatives - Neil O'Donnell, for example - and the move had its critics, but I am convinced Ron decided to gamble on experience and on Blair "coming good" on the biggest day in City's history.

Later, it was estimated that some 35,000 East Anglians made the trip to Wembley in "the biggest mass movement of people from East Anglia towards the capital since the revolt of the Iceni." Keith Skipper and I travelled to London by train and later tossed up to decide who was

*Kevin Keelan*

to phone the "live" report through to the Pink Un. I cannot remember who won, but Keith did the phoning.

It would not be an understatement to say the match was a profound disappointment for City fans, substitute Ralph Coates' 73rd minute goal sealing City's fate, for the Canaries struggled to find anything like their usual form. Perhaps it was the occasion, the 100,000 crowd, the vast, lush pitch, or the quality of the opposition, but an hour went by before they began to press Jennings into any sort of action. Still, City had made it to Wembley, the famous old stadium was bedecked with yellow and green, and that extraordinary campaign is unlikely to be forgotten by anyone who witnessed it.

Afterwards, players, officials, friends and local Press men and their wives gathered at the Portman Hotel for City's celebration banquet and dance, an altogether stranger affair with no-one quite knowing whether to suffer post-match trauma and cry or introduce an element of jollity. After all, they had lost at Wembley, and they were 21st in the League table. Anyway, we dined on minestrone au parmesane, cote de boeuf rotie and omlette

Alaska, and toasted each other with Nuits St George 1966 (I still have the tasseled menu). Later, even the Bishop of Lynn, Aubrey Aitken, a City fan for many years, joined us in the bar for a beer. The Carrow Road Press room was never like this.

*Tottenham Hotspur - Jennings; Kinnear, Knowles, Pratt, England, Beal, Gilzean, Perryman, Chivers, Peters, Pearce.*

*Norwich City - Keelan; Payne, Butler, Stringer, Forbes, Briggs, Livermore, Blair, Cross, Paddon, Anderson.*


In early March Ron Saunders paid £65,000, then the club's second highest ever fee, for Manchester City's lean and hungry-looking left-winger Ian Mellor, in a move designed to add much needed sting to the City attack. Home fans had an early opportunity to assess him when, in an unwanted diversion from the serious business of survival, the Canaries entertained Motherwell in the Texaco Cup, winning the first leg 2-0 in front of nearly 19,000 fans, including 150 visiting fans, some of whom had evidently endured a 10-hour journey by coach. City were without Livermore, Payne, Hockey, Anderson and Cross, but with Butler, Steve Goodwin, Howard and Cheesley all competing for regular places they gave a crisp performance.

The Texaco Cup was one of those pootling competitions which clubs are persuaded to take part in from time to time, though this one at least had the consolation of providing the prospect of some additional cash, because Ipswich were also competing in the final stages. Nevertheless, a few days later we all flew to Scotland to face Motherwell at home. It was a surprisingly tense encounter. The occasional harshness of some of the southern tackling raised the wrath of a highly partisan crowd, and the Scots came at City with great gusto, finally winning 3-2 thanks to a Jim McCabe hat-trick, but with City taking the final honours with a 4-3 aggregate. I remember these two encounters not only as a diversion from the leaden seriousness of the League game, but because of Motherwell's style of play, which was relaxed, attractive and, by the hurly-burly English standard of the day, slightly old fashioned.

There was little let-up in the League. City were thrashed 3-0 at White Hart Lane and dropped another point in a dire 1-1 draw against Leicester City at Carrow Road. Then they faced Liverpool at Anfield. One of City's problems had been a lack of movement and variation in attack. The system had worked well enough in Division Two and had ground out enough goals to push them towards the title, but here, in Division One, it was not enough against better class defenders. There is little doubt that Saunders had all this in mind when he chose the teams for the two Motherwell games, seeing them as an opportunity to experiment. Then a couple of days before the Anfield encounter he sprang a major surprise. Cross was out, and so was Anderson. Instead, he opted to play four in mid-field, leaving Suggett and Mellor to carry the attacking burden. The City party, with myself hovering on the fringe, arrived early at Anfield to see the place and feel something of the atmosphere, and an hour before kick-off, when the players wandered through the tunnel and on to the pitch, I went with them. At least I can claim to have done it!

The City experiment was a partial success in that there were positive signs of improvement. Even so, they lost 3-1 in front of nearly 43,000, Mellor's marvellous second half strike representing City's first away League goal in over three months.

*Liverpool - Clemence; Lawler, Lindsay, Smith, Lloyd, Hughes, Keegan, Cormack, Hall, Heighway, Callaghan.*

*Norwich City - Keelan; Butler, Black, Stringer, Forbes, Hockey, Howard, Suggett, Briggs, Paddon, Mellor.*

Easter was deemed crucial to City's survival battle, though it must be said the rest of the First Division would rather have seen them sunk without trace. Most critics dismissed them as rough, dull and sterotyped, and there was something in what they said. The criticism was too simplistic, however, for it ignored other factors, namely, what City had actually achieved, and that they were essentially a Second Division outfit struggling for First Division survival. And after all, were not Leeds dull and sterotyped when they were in Division Two, and England also, prior to their World Cup victory? There is no doubt that Saunders was hurt by all the criticism, and rightly so, leaving me in a position of being continually perplexed by the entertainment versus result dilemma of old. But there was a feeling of awe in all of it, enabling me to write at one point: "We've seen the sights this season. Been to all the posh places; mixed with the mighty. And frankly, it has been both a pleasure and an eye-opener. It is nice to know that even in these days of economic squeezes and freezes there is still a little luxury left, even though the bulk of it is restricted to Division One." Essentially, the Division One experience demonstrated just how far City had to go.

In April, City travelled to Goodison and earned a precious point after seeing a 2-0 interval lead steadily whittled away first by Belfitt and then Kendall. It left them on 26 points, with bottom club WBA on 24, and a match and several points adrift of fellow stragglers Crystal Palace, Manchester United, Stoke, Sheffield United and Birmingham. They did manage to beat Chelsea 1-0, grind out a goalless draw with WBA at the Hawthorns, and crash 3-0 at Wolverhampton. At Old Trafford, in front of 48,500 fans, Manchester United (with Stepney and Buchan, Kidd, Charlton and Law) won 1-0 to make certain of their continuing residence in Division One, but in the end all the drama of City's survival battle was telescoped into the night Crystal Palace came to Carrow Road.

Nearly 37,000 fans packed the ground for the final showdown between the two relegation contenders, and they saw Palace score first through a Don Rogers' penalty and then Colin Suggett equalise eight minutes later. It was tense, desperate stuff, with all the drama still to come. With only seconds remaining Briggs clipped a free-kick into the Palace box and David Stringer rammed the ball over the line with a powerful header. Palace, then managed by Malcom Allison, were relegated whereas City needed one more point to ensure their safety. The tension was unbearable, and at the final whistle City fans poured over the pitch, saluted their heroes, and celebrated most of the night.

*Norwich City - Keelan; C Payne, Black, Stringer, Forbes, Hockey, Livermore, Suggett, Cross, Briggs, Mellor.*

*Crystal Palace - Jackson; Mulligan, Taylor, Roffey, Blyth, Phillip, Possee, D Payne, Craven, Cooke, Rogers.*

The end, when it came, was something of an anti-climax, for it occurred not at Carrow Road but at the Hawthorns, George Lee's old haunt. Manchester City beat West Bromwich Albion 2-1 to condemn Albion to relegation, along with Crystal Palace. City were still in 20th position, but the tension drained away. Saunders was jubilant at the thought of another season in Division One, as well he might. In essence, City had only one match to go, against Stoke at the Victoria Ground, and after all the drama and heartache of the previous months it did not matter if they won or lost.

In the last few days of April, 1973, the tension drained away from me, too, for I had already decided to give up being a full-time football writer in order to follow another journalistic avenue. It was a daunting prospect. No more hours of sitting in trains - whether or not Keith Skipper was there to provide the entertainment - no more business visits to Carrow Road or Trowse, no more cups of tea in Bert Westwood's office or outings to Geoffrey Watling's office in Tombland, no more of the daily rumours and dramas, and the politics of the game. No more free tickets to matches. It was a considered decision, though, and one I had been contemplating for over a year, for after having watched over 50 matches a year for 10 or

11 years my wife was bringing up our young family while I was away, travelling to Cardiff or Charlton, Wolverhampton or Middlesbrough.

Somewhat glumly, I wrote, "Sometimes the occasional match managed to typify all that is wrong with the game: obscene chanting, violence and dissent, and an apparent disregard for order, on or off the field. This is why over the last few years many have turned their backs on it and why they watch, instead, from the safety and comfort of their own armchairs. It is a sickness, a malaise." Even so, I knew I would miss it like crazy, and in a sense still do.

So to Stoke for the final game, with Keith as travelling companion, everything relaxed and pleasant. Gordon Banks was there, visiting, waving to the crowd, while a frail-looking George Eastham managed 71 minutes of occasional flicks and passes before being replaced by another local folk hero, "Give it to 'Arry" Burrows. In the end City lost 2-0 and Saunders, away scouting, was not there to see it. But it meant very little. City were safe for another season, and it was time for me to go.

*Stoke City - Farmer; Marsh, Pejic, Mahoney, Smith, Bloor, Robertson, Greenhoff, Ritchie, Hurst, Eastham.*

*Norwich City - Keelan; Payne, Black, Stringer, Forbes, Hockey, Livermore, Suggett, Cross, Briggs, Mellor.*

# 4 Extra Time
## 1974-1997

━ ━ ━ ━ ━ ━ ━

If football had not actually become an addiction then it had certainly become a habit which proved unusually difficult, if not impossible, to break. Even today, nearly 25 years after my modest association with the game came to a full-time end, there remains the Saturday ritual of waiting for the results to appear on TV, the checking of teams, the reading of reports in the Sunday and Monday newspapers, the watching of matches on television, and irregular forays to occasional games. In a sense I have never had a personal close season, for the tentacles of that long association continue to weave a spell. In truth, the relief felt at giving up regular reporting actually emanated from a barely remembered freedom from endless travel and hotel rooms, and from the daily treadmill of football rumour, gossip, and intrigue.

In fact, in my strange, new non-football world of 1974 there were compensations in that my journalistic task involved, among other things, compiling and writing a twice (and later thrice) weekly column under the inherited name of Clement Court, a nom de plume originally pinched by the then editor of the Eastern Daily Press, Peter Roberts, from a side alley of the same name near the old offices in Redwell Street, Norwich. The essence of the old Clem column - which was allowed to die as the brave new world of the 1990s beckoned - was its Norfolkness. It had become a user-friendly, quirky repository of gossip, subjects and recollections. Before taking the job I asked Peter Roberts how he wanted it done. "Do with it as you will," he said. And for the next 13 years I did, the elbow room allowing me to develop themes, visit places and meet people of my own choosing. To be frank, it was blissful.

Late in 1975 I heard that Ron Ashman was planning a visit to Norwich, and I arranged to meet him. Since his sacking by the Canaries, whom he had first joined in 1944 and for whom he had made over 660 senior appearances, as well as having been manager, he had been boss of both

*Long Sutton's London Road ground today.*

Scunthorpe United and Grimsby Town and had just been appointed as youth scout for Lincoln City.

He had changed very little. A Cambridgeshire lad who became a Bevan boy in the pits, he was actually signed for City by Duggie Lochhead as a forward. "I was in and out of the side like a yo-yo," he recalled. "It was me and Roy Hollis for centre-forward, and one week it was me and the next, Roy. I took so much stick from the crowd that I was sick at the time." In 1948/49 he made the transition to half-back. "Bryn Jones, Len Dutton and Ivan Armes were all injured, so Norman Low shoved me in." It was as simple as that, it seems. But Ron confessed he was surprised when City ultimately offered him the acting-managership, though he was confident he could do the job. "I had learned a lot from Lochhead and Low and Archie Macaulay." Indeed, his admiration of Macaulay knew no bounds. "He could sum up 45 minutes of football and tell us at half-time exactly what to do. Or he could watch opponents and sum them up to a tee." He was less enthusiastic about the style of play fashionable throughout most of his managerial term. "The first year we finished pretty well. Then a lot of sides - Palace were one - started these defensive tactics and made it difficult to score. It reached its peak when teams came and didn't attack at all. We began to dread games, and it killed the sport for spectators for a time." But the death of Barry Butler, he felt, was the single, most significant set-back to his chances of managerial success. And the sack? "It comes as a tremendous blow. It takes a toll. But if you've been in football all your life then you know there is nothing else. There's something about the involvement, and the build-up to the Saturday that . . . well, you know."

There was a rather nice conclusion to Ron's visit. With David Challen, then landlord of the Baker's Arms pub in St Leonard's Road, I helped organise a small gathering of some of Ron's footballing friends, and am glad to record that Archie Macaulay was one of those who came along. A year later, and after many telephone calls and much letter writing, Ron came to the Baker's Arms again for a second, slightly more official club reunion. This time about 50 turned up, including club chairman Geoffrey Watling and trainer George Lee. Ron dug Billy Furness in the ribs and said, "I used to call him 'sir,'" and recalled a training session, which Billy remembered, when in his youthful enthusiasm he had called out, "Pass the ball, sir."

The former City players there that night were: Alf Kirchin (who had a remarkable City record in that, uniquely as far as I know, he was at various times a City player, coach, director and even, for a short spell following the departure of Doug Lochhead, manager), Sid Plunkett, Peter Gordon, David Stringer (then with Cambridge United), Johnny Gavin, Roy Lockwood, Tom Docherty, Joe Mann (a City goalkeeper in the 1940s), Ralph Johnson, Joe Rowell (who made his City debut at Reading in 1922), Cliff Birch (I had last seen him at Spalding), Bob Smith, Ollie Burton, Les Maskell, Albert Foan, Bob Heffer, Bryan Thurlow, John March, Roy Hollis, Derek Woodcock, Ken Shaw, Billy Furness (a City player from 1937 to 1946), Ken Nethercott, Bill Punton, Bill Brown ( like Joe Rowell, one of several ex-Canaries present who had played at Carrow Road's forerunner, the Nest, sited only a short distance from the Baker's Arms, and who then lived a mere stone's throw from the old battleground ), Tim Williamson (who joined the Canaries in 1930/31 and was Stoke City's centre-half when a lad named Stanley Matthews signed for the Potters), Terry Allcock, Ron Ashman, Bill Lewis, Mike Sutton (then a teacher in Norwich), Sid Jones, Les Eyre (who shared digs with Ashman when Ron first came to Norwich), Albert Bennett, Maurice Tobin, Jimmy Moran, Ron Hansell and Jim Oliver.

It was not the end of this particular story. In 1985 David Challen, who by this time had moved to the Kingsway pub in Lakenham, organised yet another reunion. Again, about 50 turned up, including Ralph Wright, Clive Payne, Trevor Painter, Sandy Kennon, George Morgan, Derrick Lythgoe, Martin Peters (of World Cup fame), Bill Lewis, Billy Steele, Bill Punton,

Terry Woodcock, Ollie Burton, Peter Gordon, Bob Heffer, Roy Lockwood, Alan Bullimore, Derek Woodcock, Ron Hansell, Cliff Birch, Peter Applegate, Ron Ashman, Jim Robson, Alf Kirchin, Gren Williams, Ron Bacon, Les Maskell, Peter Tough, Bill Cleary, Alan Arber, Tim Williamson, Bill Brown, Chris Watts, Bert Holmes, Ken Nethercott, Ralph Johnson, Duncan Forbes, Steve Govier, Albert Bennett, Peter Silvester, Phil Kelly, Russell Laskey, Graham Willis, Maurice Tobin, Mike Tolley, Noel Gilbert and Terry Allcock. Former secretary Bert Westwood also popped in to say, "Hello."

*The modern outline of Norwich City's Carrow Road ground.*

Crowd violence has always hovered at the edges of the game, and there is no point in pretending otherwise. While it was possible in 1955 for one writer to describe soccer crowds as being as "orderly as church meetings," and while the terraces do seem to have enjoyed a relatively peaceful spell just before and just after the second world war, the potential for trouble has always been present. Asa Briggs (A Social History of England. BCA, 1994) quoted Phillip Stubbes, a 16th century Puritan, as complaining that football - which locally was probably called camping, hence Camping or Camp Hills - was more "a freendly kynde of fight" than a recreation, while another dismissed the game as "nothing but beastly fury and extreme violence." Even the EDP reported in its 100 Years Ago column, in November, 1995, that at Lakenham in 1895 a visiting player had been kicked and punched by a disorderly crowd and the referee escorted to the pavilion by a bodyguard after he had disallowed a "goal" by the home side.

Certainly the 1960s engendered its share of troubles, on and off the pitch, which in part I am sure was due to a slow erosion of personal responsibilities, drunken indiscipline, a new and frightening culture of violence, and an inexorable rise in monetary reward. But few incidents can have been so frightening — and as a paying spectator at the game I speak from personal experience - as that which occurred at Carrow Road on Saturday, April 22, 1977, when Manchester United were the visitors and television cameras were present, either because they wanted to assess whether United's fans were as distructively violent as their reputation suggested or because they had a hunch that mayhem, as well as football, might be on the agenda that day.

Shortly before 2pm I walked with a swarm of fans by Thorpe railway station and along Riverside. United supporters were pouring across the station forecourt, and a noisy trek towards Carrow Road began. Police and film crews were everywhere. A TV crew filmed the United fans, and they reacted noisily and animatedly. Then police vans began to shadow the column, and the TV crew picked up its bits and pieces and gave chase. A blue and white Transit van, its back doors open a few inches, followed the police vans. Less publicly, in the rear of the Transit van, a police cameraman squatted behind the partially open doors and began to film a long, orderly column of largely middle-aged City supporters. The two huge streams of fans finally merged at Carrow Bridge and the roadway was a sea of shuffling people. The TV crew had repositioned itself beside the River End turnstiles, and the Transit van and its crew edged towards the police entrance beside the Barclay Stand. They began to unload film gear.

Inside the Barclay stand there was an unmistakeable air of menace. Two armies screamed and gestured at each other across the no-man's land of a middle pen deserted save for a possee of policemen and women. Two tall webs of iron railings guarded the demarcation lines. But at about 2.30pm, and presumably because a crush of United fans was still waiting to get in - the crowd that day was just over 26,000 - the police suddenly decided to open the middle section. A red and white horde poured in. Now the two sets of fans could get to grips with each other, a single set of railings and some increasingly anxious police officers keeping them apart. There was an unceasing barrage of insults and a lot of spitting and scuffling. Some red and white clad infiltrators tried to climb the fence, and a few succeeded only to be grabbed, in an armlock or by the hair, and hustled out. There was a lot of kicking and scrambling, and tension was rising fast.

The first serious violence occurred at 2.40pm, inside the City pen. A group of United followers who had been standing quietly and anonymously at the back suddenly hurled themselves down the concrete terraces into the heart of the City territory. The crowd panicked and cascaded downhill, spilling on to the pitch. Young and old tumbled and fell, and there was much scrambling, shoving and screaming. Then harrassed policemen darted in to deal with the injured, and a degree of sanity returned. Two or three yards away from me three policemen struggled with a youth who was lashing out with his feet. One policeman kicked back. Another took off his helmet and used it to belabour the youth. He was dragged away still struggling.

Five minutes before kick-off United manager Tommy Docherty, surrounded by cameramen, appeared on the pitch in front of the Barclay Stand and made a brave but largely ignored gesture for peace. His actual words were lost in the hubbub. And at 3.07pm City scored, through Suggett. For a time it quietened the crowd but some City youths, growing in confidence, began to taunt their opposite numbers. There was a spell of coin throwing, and a heavy glass Ben Truman ash tray sailed through the air and shattered harmlessly at the back. Occasional attempts by both sets of fans were made to get through the railings, and police "snatch squads" periodically darted into the ruck and hauled someone off.

As the game progressed United's fans became increasingly vindictive. There was another hail of beer cans, and bloodied heads appeared on both sides of the railings. Then at about 4.10pm the red and white army made its first concerted attempt to dislodge the railings. Dozens of them clasped the iron bars and began to move them too and fro. The bars wobbled alarmingly and some were uprooted from their concrete footings. But the barrier held. So they tried something else. One group had the idea of going out of the back of the stand and trying to get into the City pen from behind. A padlocked, wooden door at the rear was rattled and kicked. A inquisitive policeman quietly unlocked the door and peered out. Suddenly it burst inwards, knocking his helmet askew. A snatch squad poured out in pursuit and the door was hastily re-locked. Now the police were under constant pressure. There was fighting all over the Barclay terraces, and scrambling figures. Rubbish and missiles flew back and forth and police uniforms glistened with spittle.

At 4.30pm, with the final whistle approaching, the bulk of the police at the back of the stand moved away to duties outside the ground, until only the bars and a thin blue line separated the warring factions.When the whistle finally went City fans again taunted the United fans, and another hail of coins streamed over the barrier. The loudspeakers pleaded for City fans to wait while the United fans left the ground; but the opposite occurred. As City's supporters slowly shuffled towards the exits, hundreds of visitors attacked the railings with renewed vigour. A few red and white infiltrators manage to climb over, and there are not enough police to hold them back. At that point a serious clash seemed inevitable, for the exits were choked, the City fans were unable to get away, and United supporters were advancing on all sides. There was another concerted attempt to batter down the padlocked door. A couple of policemen put their shoulders against it, but the iron stanchions bent alarmingly. Then there was the sound of a large-scale attack on the entire timbered rear section of the Barclay stand, which echoed with bangs and crashes and the sound of splintering wood. More police arrived, this time with truncheons drawn, but the hammering, smashing and splintering went on as hundreds of City fans, trapped against the choked exits, turned to meet the inevitable attack. The wooden section finally shattered and the police hurled themselves into the gaps to try to hold the United fans back. There was a furious battle. Slats of broken wood and debris rained into the packed roadway outside the ground. As I was swept away by the frightened tide towards the comparative safety of Carrow Bridge I glanced back towards the Barclay. The iron railings were badly damaged and the timbered rear of the stand was largely destroyed. More significantly, a line of policemen and women, a thin, brave blue strand stretched across the terraces, was managing to hold hundreds of United fans at bay as City's supporters poured out of the exits towards the comparative safety of the city's streets.

Later estimates suggested there were 6500 United supporters at the game and 280 police on duty at the ground. About 30 spectators and eight policemen were injured; there were 19 arrests; six nearby homes and several parked cars were damaged, and many windows broken; a small fire was started; and the Barclay stand was sorely vandalised. City won, however, and there were some exciting crowd pictures on television.

*Norwich City - Keelan; Ryan, Sullivan, Machin, Jones, Powell, Neighbour, Reeve, Gibbins, Suggett, Peters.*

*Manchester United - Stepney; Nicholl, Houston, McIlroy, B Greenhoff, Buchan, Coppell, J Greenhoff, McCreery, Macari, Hill.*

I must confess to slight regret that I never saw the game in the 1920/30s, but only towards the end of the so-called "golden" age, if there ever was such a thing. Pre-television tales of legendary players performing in front of unimaginably huge crowds are buried deep in the sporting psyche, and it has long been thus. Again, Asa Briggs (A Social History of England. BCA, 1994) recorded that one observer in an industrial town in 1898 noted that every fragment of overheard conversation was "a piece of football criticism or prophecy." Only 30 or 40 years before this the game had moved from rural fields and grimy back alleys to the public schools, whence goal sizes were determined (was the width really the average length of three

*Spalding United's ground today has a smart new grandstand.*

men in 1868?) and rules formulated. By the end of the century, however, it had been re-possessed by the people who had first taken an interest in it.

In late August, 1983, and almost exactly 75 years to the day when it was first mooted, I puffed my way up St Matthew's Hill in Norwich in search of what was left of the Canaries' old ground, the Nest. City had been using a pitch in Newmarket Road for many years, but facilities for the players and duckboards and wooden benches for the crowds scarcely mirrored the club's real ambition or potential. In 1907/08, for example, over 10,000 spectators turned up to see City take on Sheffield Wednesday. It was farmer and dairyman John Pyke, the club chairman, who finally led the initiative. During the summer of 1908 he acquired a disused chalkpit in Rosary Road, handily close to the busy railway station, and engaged a huge labour force to transform it into what was to become the club's home for the next 27 years. They filled the gravel pit, smoothed the surface, put down grass, built fences and erected terracing where space and terrain allowed. Most impressive of all was the construction of a massive concrete retaining wall, 30ft to 50ft high in places, in the angle of one of the corners. The rampart propped up a cliff which in turn supported rows of terraced houses, and gave the Nest its distinctive look and atmosphere. When the ground finally opened it was a pinched arena cut into a precipitous hillside made of thin soil, sand and chalk, surrounded on three sides by steep slopes. Little more than a hole in the side of a hill, in fact.

Old photographs give something of the flavour of the place. The crowds swarmed along Riverside, St Matthew's, St Leonard's and Rosary Roads and clung like ants to the terraces and slopes. A squat, wooden grandstand ran along one portion of the touchline; the players, at least in the early days, wore knee length knickers, huge leather boots, and shirts laced at the collar; while above them towered the slopes of the Nest and the rooftops of Thorpe Hamlet. These were the days of Beale and Hampson, Pompey Martin and Tricky Hawes, Jobling and Williamson, when visiting wingers were "skinned" against the fearsome wall a mere foot or two from the touchline, when cash crisis followed cash crisis, and when crowds of over 20,000 managed to cling to the slopes. In 1922 a stretch of terracing crumbled and 50 fans were spilled from the top of the wall. And in 1934 over 25,000 turned up for an FA Cup-tie, again against Sheffield Wednesday, with another 5000 unable to get in. Something had to be done. The Nest had became known by its detractors as "Pyke's folly," and for the second time in its short history the Canaries were being held back by inadequate and even unsafe facilities.

One final recollection of the old ground, recounted much later by Russell Allison, the then Carrow Road groundsman, whose father was also groundsman at the Nest. One day a large hole appeared in the Rosary Road end of the pitch, which investigation showed was 20ft deep. Russell's father told him that, with an important match due only a couple of days later, they filled in the hole with rubble, lay railway sleepers over the top, and replaced the turf. Before the match the players were told to be careful when they took corners. Finally, in 1935, with the League threatening to close them down, the club moved to Carrow Road, an episode worthy of a book of its own.

In 1983 the old Nest, disused for sport for many years, was covered by concrete buildings. Most of the terracing was gone, too, but the dark slopes remained, sheltered by trees and bushes, as did the great wall. At the rear of Bertram Books' warehouse it still rose to a frightening height, walkways and railings crumbling and rusty, its outlines softened by greenery. There were traces of flaking paint and I could still pick out one of the old advertisements - "Drink milk and keep fit" - perhaps Pyke-inspired. And close to Rosary Road, not far from where Russell Allison senior filled in the hole and trod back the turf there was a few feet of spike-topped ornamental railing and a sad, short, desolate stretch of concrete terracing, mottled with moss and under attack from sycamore. But enough to clamber on, stretch your legs, and try to conjure the scene.

In the early 1980s, too, Charlton's difficulties began to surface, though truth to tell the clues had been waiting to be read for much longer. I recalled sitting amid the Charlton Press seats a decade earlier looking sorrowfully at the decay, at the struggling team, and at a 12,000 attendance all but swallowed by the vastness, and wondering: how much longer? As it happened my very last visit to the old Valley was to see Manchester City in December, 1984, by which time the decline looked irreversible. Up the steps from the station, over the bridge and into Floyd Road, and there it was, in all its faded dereliction. The Valley, that huge concrete bowl with its tiny main stand, the source of so much of my youthful inspiration, had become an albatross; the terraces, once the club's pride and joy where 70,000 had stood and sang and swelled with pride, were now its downfall. The place looked untidy and sad, its downward progress apparently out of control. Conclusive proof of the scale of decline was to be found in the match programme that day. The last four home gates had been 4073, 4841, 6950 and 3744.

A few months earlier the club - though not the ground - had been sold, but in August, 1985, Greater London Council closed the crumbling East Terrace in response to the Heysel and Bradford disasters and calls for tighter safety regulations. A few weeks after that the club gave notice of moving to Selhurst Park to ground-share with Crystal Palace. Charlton fans were horrified. But what, I wondered, was the alternative? Had they stayed at the Valley the only option was oblivion. Yet the fans demonstrated and newspaper writers compiled epitaphs to the Valley.

Frank Keating wrote that Charlton, a major force in war-time football, "was one of the first household names that seeped into the conciousness of even we rugger-bred tots in a Gloucestershire village." David Lacey commented that while "Charlton Athletic are the Woolwich Ferry, the Greenwich loop line and the Blackwall Tunnel approach, Crystal Palace are Norwood Junction and Thornton Heath Pond. Charlton are Thames Estuary and North Kent; Palace are Croydon and the A23." They all remembered dear old Sam Bartram, the club's war-time and post-war hero, and the Valley, which in 1938 held 75,000 for an FA Cup-tie against Aston Villa. The Guardian, in a tearful leader, wrote in September, 1985: "Stand on top of the East Terrace and, even if the football gladiators far below are having a bad day, the panorama across dockland is one of the great sights of London. There's a sense of history in the higgledy-piggledy mix of spare acres, 50-year-old stands and the goals that Sam Bartram once defended. When the sun shines it's one of the most endearing grounds in the land; when a storm crackles over the Thames, you watch the Twilight of the Gods from a natural balcony."

Back home in Norfolk I asked the readers of my column in the EDP if there were any Charlton fans among them. The final tally was five-and-a-half: myself, and readers in Trimingham, Lowestoft, Wicklewood and Norwich. The half represented a man declared by his wife to be "a Charlton supporter sometimes." One correspondent, describing me as a "rookie supporter," asked pointedly, "Where were you in 1923 when, in Charlton's first entry into the FA Cup, we beat Manchester City, Preston and West Brom, only to lose 1-0 to Bolton when David Jack scored? As I tell Norwich supporters - suffering? They don't know the meaning of the word." Unborn in 1923, I am not quite certain where I was. But I understood the sentiment.

*Charlton Athletic - Johns; Curtis, Friar, Gritt, Moore, Berry, Towner, Hales, Lee, Aizlewood, Flanagan.*

*Manchester City - Williams; May, Power, Reid, McCarthy, Phillips, Smith, Baker, Melrose, Wilson, Kinsey.*


Much of the Lennie Lawrence era with Charlton passed me by in a sense that I saw little of the side, as did the challenging Hales and Flanagan period. Lennie was manager for nine extraordinary years, the second longest spell in the club's history, and I have never fully understood how he achieved what he did. First, he had to deal with the economic ruin of the club, the loss of its ground, and its re-siting in alien territory. Yet with little or no cash available he vigorously re-built the side, got them into Division One (when it was the proper Division One) and kept them there for a spell, and then, when he left the club in 1991 to join Middlesbrough, he handed over a team in a much stronger state than when he started. For my money he was Manager of the Year for several years in a row, though I suppose it depends how you interpret success. Managers at Old Trafford, Anfield and Highbury are expected to be in Division One (or nowadays, the Premiership) and win Cups and titles, and usually have bagfulls of money to throw at a problem should it occur. Lennie was supposed to be in Division Two (or even Three), not expected to win anything, and had little or no money. And yet he kept the club alive, got them into Division One, and even got them to Wembley. I know which sort of achievement I prefer.

Having said that, the Wembley appearance was a disaster. In 1987 Charlton won their way through to the final of the Football League Full Members' Cup, beating Birmingham City, Bradford City, Everton and, emotionally and somewhat dramatically, Norwich City, which lined them up to meet Blackburn Rovers on the hallowed turf. This was something not to be missed. I managed to scrounge a ticket and thus sat once again in the Wembley Press box. Despite the prestige, the occasion, and a 40,000 crowd, only a small percentage of which were displaying red favours, Charlton looked as though the cares of the world had finally descended upon their shoulders. They lost 1-0, somewhat unfortunately, though in truth they never looked good enough to win.

*Blackburn Rovers - O'Keefe; Price, Sulley, Barker, Keeley, Mail, Miller, Ainscow, Hendry, Garner, Sellars.*

*Charlton Athletic - Bolder; Humphrey, Reid, Peake, Thompson, Miller, Milne, Lee, Melrose, Walsh, Shipley.*

The history of a football club is measured by landmarks which, more often than not, are followed by periods of retrenchment or decline. For all

*Smart new stands have replaced the old terraces at Charlton's Valley ground.*

but the monied, these landmarks are usually few and far between. However, Norwich City clearly reached a major one in the giant, fog enshrouded and clatteringly cold San Siro stadium, Milan, on December 8, 1993, when they were beaten 1-0 (2-0 on aggregate) in the UEFA Cup by Inter Milan thanks to a goal by Bergkamp, who cost Inter more than the entire City team cost Carrow Road. But for some reason the result hardly seemed to matter.

This match was City's statement that they had arrived. Having beaten Vitesse Arnhem and Bayern Munich in earlier rounds, and held Inter to a single goal at Carrow Road, City were, to the Italians and the European soccer world at large, little known upstarts who warrented no more than a 30,000 atttendance rattling and echoing around beneath the famous Milanese portals. But this, I feel, was City's Cup Final, a signal that memories of the 1950s Cup run, or even Old Trafford in 1967, had been put behind them and that they had carved their own, modern niche in club history. The fact that manager Mike Walker and half the team, including Fox, Sutton and Ekoku, were to leave shortly afterwards, though a commentary on club economic policy at the time, is very largely an irrelevance as far as the San Siro was concerned. City's supporters had been to the temple of the mighty, played Inter Milan on Italian soil, and had turned in a performance certainly as good and as brave as anything I had seen from a City side, Highbury, Stamford Bridge and Old Trafford notwithstanding.

After the final whistle the City fans had their say, making an emotive, 30-minute vocal statement in the otherwise empty stadium. Clap, clap, clap, clap. "NC-FC, NC-FC. Wal-ker's Ar-my, Wal-ker's Ar-my." Clap, clap, clap, clap. On and on it went, a fast, rhymical expression of the joy at being there, an act which signalled the end of the club's age of innocence. The Inter fans had disappeared as soon as the final whistle sounded, but stadium staff stayed to watch and listen, at first wary and watchful, perhaps anticipating trouble, then incredulous, until finally they joined in, too. And after half an hour we filed out, leaving the San Siro to its echoing aloofness and the fog. Norfolk farmer's sons and villagers shook hands with smiling Italian terrace sweepers and groundsmen, and slapped each other on the back. Grazi, grazi. There was honour even in being there, even in defeat, because this new generation of City fans could now talk about Munich and Milan instead of having to endure tales of ancient derring-do against Tottenham and Luton and the Busby Babes.

The return flight from Malpensa airport to Norwich was also memorable, hilarious and truly alarming, for storm winds approaching hurricane force battered the Boeing 747 all the way home, causing it to buck and rear and do all manner of wildly unpleasant things. The cheerfulness of this particular "load of turkey farmers" could not be blown away, however. There was a marvellously irreverent safety demonstration before take-off, when every move by the stewardess at the front of the fuselage was greeted with riotous applause. Yellow and green balloons were batted up and down the narrow aisle in a frenzy of childish delight, and the fans sang, "Always look on the bright side of life," and after a particularly envigorating spell of rearing and bucking, "We always sing when we're frightened." Every pitch and roll was cheered, and amid the buffeting a chap in the seat in front turned to his neighbour and said, "It feels like some of Charlie's asphalting." Even the flight crew must have heard the huge cheer which arose when, after a hair-raising approach in the teeth of the wind, the aircraft's wheels finally slammed into the runway at Norwich airport.

*The scene as Norwich City take the field at the San Siro ground in Milan.*

*Inter Milan - Zenga; Battistini, Orlando, Bergomi, M Paganin, A Paganin,
Shalimov, Dell'Anno, Fontalan, Bergkamp, Sosa.*
    *Norwich City - Gunn; Bowen, Newman, Prior, Woodthorpe, Fox, Megson,
Goss, Ullathorne, Sutton, Ekoku.*


Football, and the business of football, have both changed in 50 years
and there is no getting away from it. If you require from me a judgement
which says that, 50 years on, it is better or worse, then you will not get it.
I will go no further than to say that it is different, in a number of ways.
From my perspective there have been several Ages of the game. We are
now at the start of the fourth.
    The first age, I think, was the *Fairytale Age* of huge crowds and legendary
stars when the football was, in a sense, carefree, alive and exciting, perhaps
a little smug, insulated in its own world, the poor man's game and the
poor man's weekly dose of excitement and entertainment, when the
players received next to nothing and the clubs lived on gate money. The
second period, the *Nervous Age,* began about 1956 and lasted until about
1970, when economics began to bite, attendances fell, players' salaries

went up and neither clubs nor managers quite knew what the future held, commercially or tactically. To be frank it was also a glum, evolutionary time, when the gentlemanly amateur status finally fell by the wayside and teams learned the rudiments of how not to lose by stopping the other chap playing. The third phase, from about 1970 to about 1990, must be called the *Showbiz Age*, not only because of George Best and Carnaby Street, dolly birds, long hair, fashion, gold chains on manly chests, glitz and the Chelsea set, but also because, thanks to television, of the slow evolution of top managers and top players from folk heroes into showbiz personalities. And the fourth, from about 1990 to some date in the future? I suppose this has to be the *Commercial Age*, a time of flotations, share dealings, marketing managers, brand images and boardroom battles. So far, to be fair, it has produced at the top of the tree the Premiership (an enormous commercial success), some fine new grounds, and a divided game already showing signs of economic distress at root level. The jury is still out on this one.

Tactically, 1966 represented a watershed of sorts just as Hungary's defeat of England - or the manner of it - in the 1950s stopped everyone in their tracks and forced a major tactical re-think. The early 1960s, of course, represented the dying gasp of the old post-war football ethos, with its unashamed joy, huge popularity, and insular style and attitudes. From the mid- and late-1960s, however the public watched a different sort of game. No longer could a winger or a ball player find space in which to express himself, or the inside-forward time to put his foot on the ball and then produce an unexpected pass of great beauty. Time and space were squeezed and compressed; pace overcame expression, workrate crushed creativity, and organisation killed off improvisation. It was often painful and sometimes indescribably dull.

Oddly, there seem to be fewer deliberately boring games than there used to be (in the late 1960s some teams did not want to win, simply avoid defeat), merely occasional bad ones. Perhaps the advent of three points for a win, advocated by me back in the early 1970s I am happy to say, has had something to do with that. And there seems to be a new determination in the game to win back and hold its audience. There are even lounges, seats and proper toilets at Carrow Road and at the Valley. Back in 1960 all that, along with scampi and chips, would have been thought of as radically bourgeois. So there have been changes and plusses.

All changes elicit a price, so what of the minuses? Well, the divisions are still too large, the England squad is still not given a sufficiently high priority, and traditional, historical and social links with host communities have been weakened to a degree. Twenty-five years ago no-one would have

*The home of the Tigers - Carter's Park, Holbeach. It is very largely
unchanged, even after 40 years.*

dared talk about ownership, because it was assumed clubs were "owned,"
spiritually and morally if not financially, by their supporting communities.
Chairman were figureheads, grand, shadowy figures who looked after
the paperwork and made occasional announcements. Now chairmen,
business managers, financial managers and marketing managers have
evolved as a powerful elite. Players are marketing opportunities, grounds
are real estate, profits and share values are everything, while
entrepreneurial board members have become personalities in their own
right. Some would say the cart is beginning to push the horse. Certainly I
prefer things on a smaller, more homely scale.
   As for the game on the pitch a few things do seem to be happening after
a long slumber, tactically speaking, during most of the 1980s. Having said
that, playing only three defenders at the back can hardly be said to be
hugely innovatory. I do like the pace and the robustness of the modern
game - it is interesting what Glen Hoddle and later, Ruud Gullit, attempted
at Chelsea - though I miss the theatrical spectacle of packed, towering
terraces, and I miss the unexpected. In my book one creative pass from

Brooking (or today, perhaps, Matt Le Tissier, Di Matteo, Zola or Cantona) was worth two midfielders displaying 100% workrates. But I do dislike the dissent, and often wonder if soccer needs a sin bin system or a rule under which sides concede 10 yards if they argue with the referee; the jumping for high balls with elbows up and out instead of by the side; two-footed tackling or tackling from the back or the side and certainly not shoulder to shoulder; and the awful back-pass rule which forces goalkeepers into ugly fly-kick clearances.

Off the field, with power vested in the men with the money, my feeling is that football needs to proceed warily on two or three fronts. First, there is surely danger in travelling too far along the path of supplying everything that television demands. Fixture dates, FA Cup draws and kick-off times are already arranged to suit programming needs. Requests for larger goalmouths, the abolition of drawn games, and time-outs for advertising breaks may already be in the pipeline for all I know. Then there is the question of separation. There may come a time (perhaps together with some of the larger Scottish clubs such as Rangers, Celtic and Aberdeen) when the Premiership will seek to detach itself altogether from the Nationwide League in order to float free in its own self-important, highly inflated atmosphere, its life support systems primed by squillions of pounds pumped in by competing satellite, cable and pay-as-you-view networks and the BBC and current commercial channels. The reality is that any damage to the lower divisions must, by definition, damage the game as a whole. If the Premiership is not one day to obtain all its players from abroad, then it needs the Nationwide divisions just as much as Nationwide clubs need the Premiership.

A more equal distribution of the game's commercial wealth, and not further separation, is surely the most sensible way to prevent some clubs in the lower divisions withering away or turning part-time. After all, an industry which relies on peripheral funding must always be vulnerable. What would happen if club shop sales declined, or if television, because of a policy change or out of boredom, suddenly turned its back on football in favour of some "new" upstart sport, possibly from America. Unlikely? Well, it can happen. Ask showjumping.

Finally, there is the question of admission charges. In the 1960s we judged the viability of terrace ticket increases at Carrow Road by comparing the cost with the price of a seat at the Odeon. For years the two tickets maintained a sort of parity. At the time of writing the cost of soccer has moved way ahead, roughly, £5 at the cinema and £10 at Carrow Road. If City get promotion again the disparity will increase even further. What has been gained by placing this enormous additional burden on the shoulders of supporters? Higher salaries for players and background staff. Improved facilities. Executive boxes? Of dubious value to real fans. A seat? Possibly, though having endured the discomfort that goes with some of these narrow, cramped plastic contraptions, I have yet to be convinced they are always an advantage. But a warning light is there. The supporter can afford only so much. Complete reliance on high admission charges merely increases the desperation ratio if form deserts the team and gates do start to fall.

Of "my" five clubs, Carrow Road and the Valley have changed the most, the Halley Stewart and Long Sutton somewhat, and Carter's Park

*The view from the Press bench at Carter's Park, Holbeach.*

hardly at all. At Long Sutton the ground has been emasculated and new building encroaches on to the area where the old pitch and grandstand used to be. The present pitch is on its later site, closer to London Road, and is surrounded by moveable metal crowd barriers many of which, on the day I called, had been re-arranged by the same frolicksome element I presume had also damaged the little touchline shelters. But at least the club has new dressing rooms, a car park, and floodlights, hoisted high on four corner pedestals.

The skyline at Spalding's trim and pleasant Halley Stewart playing field is still dominated by the same shabby, giant water tower. In my day is used to glower over the bus station; now it is a backdrop for supermarkets and shopping areas. As for the ground, it has the same secluded air, hidden behind its protective walls, and the same covered terrace behind the town end goal, though an attempt has been made to put seats in the middle block. And it, too, has floodlights, first switched on in 1980 when, once again, Norwich City were the visitors. The big change, however, is that the old dressing rooms and the wooden Press box have been swept away and replaced by the Tulips' Social Club and a furniture store, and a very smart, neat brick grandstand.

Even the wooden grandstand still remains at Holbeach even if the dressing rooms have been replaced and the ticket office and phone booth have gone. And there are floodlights, here, too. In fact the last time I called in, when I was totally alone save for two children on bikes on the far side of the park, I sat once again on my old wooden Press seat, looked at the empty pitch and the deserted stand - somehow smaller and shabbier than I remembered - the advertising billboards on the railings, and recalled with gratitude Richley and Tootill, Watkins and Fox, Megginson and Sharman, Anderson and Nicholson, the rattles and black and yellow scarves, touchlines thronged with fans and "Tiger Rag" blaring from the loudspeakers. I had also forgotten how narrow was the stretch of grass between the railings and the touchline, and how close the players were to the fans. Perhaps that was part of the magic.

To be honest it was with a sense of foreboding that I first made my way to Charlton's new ground in March, 1995, to see the Portsmouth game, only to be quite bowled over by its bright cheerfulness, its compactness, and the fresh energy it seemed to have injected into the club. Same pitch, on which Sam played his heart out season after season, different surroundings; and I could not dispel a feeling of astonishment that, after all that had happened, not only was there a new Valley but the club was still in business.

And Carrow Road? In November, 1996, when Charlton came to town, I sat in the River End, top deck, and looked across the pitch towards the heights of Thorpe Hamlet in the misty distance. Here, too, the changes have been profound. Macaulay and Ashman, Morgan and Davies, Russell Allison and Ron Saunders, they would remember the South Stand, though it now has seats rather than terraces, but little else. The rest of the ground is crisp and modern. I could not even work out where the new Press box was situated.

*Charlton Athletic - Salmon; Brown, Mortimore, Jones, Rufus, Balmer, Robson, Leaburn, Pardew, Whyte, Robinson.*

*Portsmouth - Knight; Gittens, Russell, McLoughlin, Symonds, Butters, Pethick, Preki, Hall, Creaney, Powell.*


February 22, 1997. Charlton Athletic versus Norwich City in the Nationwide Division One. It rounded off my 50 years. More or less, anyway. But near enough to mean something. Circle Line tube to Charing Cross and then suburban train from the very same platform I first used in 1951. And the same stations. London Bridge, Deptford, Greenwich, Maze Hill, Westcombe Park, then Charlton. The same platform, up the same steps, and across the same bridge. Left into Floyd Road, stroll by Sam's old shop. Purchase a match ticket at the spanking new

*Sam's spirit lives on at the Valley.*

box office behind the Jimmy Seed Stand not far from a block of flats where a road sign proclaims Sam Bartram Close. Later, buy a programme in the club shop and wander back along Charlton Church Lane for a pint of Bass in the The Antigallican, the pub on the corner. The programme talks grandly of impending Stock Exchange flotation and of a dinner/dance at London's Cafe Royal to mark the 50th anniversary of the Addicks winning the FA Cup. Is it really that long ago?

   As for the match, it was an eight-goal thriller, watched by nearly 13,000 fans in the bright, compact, re-born Valley. Afterwards, I share a packed train back to Charing Cross with a new generation of disgruntled Norwich City fans bemoaning the loss of two more points. Still hoping, still grumbling. Like all of us, still sharing the dream.

   *Charlton Athletic - Petterson; Brown, Chapple, Balmer, Barness, Robson, K Jones, Kinsella, Robinson, S Jones, Lee.*

   *Norwich City - Gunn; Newman, Crook, Mills, Adams, Johnson, Milligan, Rocastle, Sutch, Ottosson, Eadie.*

FINAL WHISTLE